New
Old-Fashioned
Ways

Old-

CINCORITA

Margarita Of The Mon...

New Fashíoned Ways

Holidays and Popular Culture

Jack Santino

The University of Tennessee Press / Knoxville

"All Summer Long" by Brian Wilson. Copyright 1964, renewed 1992, Irving Music, Inc. (BMI) All rights reserved. Intl. copyright secured. Used by permission.

"The Circle Game," words and music by Joni Mitchell. © 1966 (Renewed) Crazy Crow Music (BMI). All Rights Reserved. Used by Permission. WARNER BROS. PUBLICATIONS U.S. INC., Miami, FL 33014.

"Hello Mudduh, Hello Fadduh (A Letter from Camp)" words by Allan Sherman, music by Lou Busch. Copyright 1963, renewed 1991, Curtain Call Production/Burning Bush Music. Used by permission. All rights reserved.

"Lost in the Stars," by Maxwell Anderson and Kurt Weill. © 1944, 1946 (Copyrights Renewed) TRO Hampshire House Publishing Corp. & Chappell & Co. All Rights Reserved. Used by Permission. WARNER BROS. PUBLICATIONS U.S. INC., Miami, FL 33014.

"River," words and music by Joni Mitchell. © 1971, Joni Mitchell Publishing Corp. All Rights Reserved. Used by Permission. WARNER BROS. PUBLICATIONS U.S. INC., Miami, FL 33014.

"Rockin' Around the Christmas Tree." Copyright 1958 St. Nicholas Music, Inc. Renewed 1986. All Rights Reserved.

"Sealed with a Kiss," words by Peter Udell, music by Gary Geld. © 1960 (Renewed) EMI U Catalog Inc. All Rights Reserved. Used by Permission. WARNER BROS. PUBLICATIONS U.S. INC., Miami, FL 33014.

"Sisters of Mercy" written by Leonard Cohen. Copyright 1967 Bad Monk Publishing. Used by permission. All rights reserved.

"Summertime," words and music by George Gershwin, DuBose and Dorothy Heyward, and Ira Gershwin. © 1935 (Renewed) George Gershwin Music, Ira Gershwin Music, and DuBose and Dorothy Heyward Memorial Fund. All Rights administered by WB Music Corp. All Rights Reserved. Used by Permission. WARNER BROS. PUBLICATIONS U.S. INC., Miami, FL 33014.

"Summertime Blues," by Eddie Cochran and Jerry Capehart. © 1958 (Renewed) Warner-Tamerlane Publishing Corp. (BMI). All Rights Reserved. Used by Permission. WARNER BROS. PUBLICATIONS U.S. INC., Miami, FL 33014.

"Urge for Goin'" words and music by Joni Mitchell. © 1966 (Renewed) Crazy Cajun Music. All Rights Reserved. Used by Permission. WARNER BROS. PUBLICATIONS U.S. INC., Miami, FL 33014.

The paper in this book meets the minimum requirements of the American National Standard for Permanence of Paper for Printed Library Materials. ∞ The binding materials have been chosen for strength and durability.

Printed on recycled paper.

Library of Congress Cataloging-in-Publication Data

Santino, Jack.
New old-fashioned ways : holidays and popular culture / Jack
    Santino. —1st ed.
        p.   cm.
    Includes bibliographical references (p.) and index.
    ISBN 0-87049-952-1 (pbk. : alk. paper)
    1. Holidays. 2. Popular culture. I. Title.
GT3930.S26 1996
394.2'6—dc20   96-9993
                        CIP

For my mother,

Mrs. Anna J. Kiley Santino

Contents

Illustrations

Acknowledgments

This is the most fattening book I have ever written. Collecting holiday-oriented beer, cookies, candy, and snack foods has its risks. Moreover, purchasing those items, along with comic books, paperbacks, and compact disks, has been expensive. But most of all, it has been fun. This book is the result of many tidbits of information, of people's generosity in bringing to my attention items they thought I might be interested in. In many ways it is (like all books, I suspect) a group effort. I owe Marjorie McKinstry for the Cinco Rita, Jacko Rita, and Santa Rita materials. Kerry Lamare gave me the Mardi Gras potato chips, which I ate before having the bag photographed. Professor William L. Schurk, sound recordings archivist for the Bowling Green State University Popular Music Collection, provided access to a wealth of holiday-oriented albums. David Dupont helped me out with the lyrics to "Lost in the Stars." All photographs were taken by David Hampshire, of Bowling Green State University. Colleen Coughlin opened my eyes to *The Nightmare Before Christmas*. I have included the work of one of my students, Stacy Young, in the text, but I want to express special thanks to her for her good work. Many people warned me that securing song lyric permissions would be very difficult and unpleasant, but this task was handled with grace and efficiency by Margaret Weinberger. I doubt that I would have been able to complete the book without her work, and I wish to express my gratitude to her and to all the above-named friends and colleagues.

Meredith Morris-Babb at the University of Tennessee Press has been delightful throughout the entire process, always supportive and encouraging. My thanks to her. Thanks also to Thomas Zimmerman for all his good work.

My children probably loved this project even more than I did, especially when they visited my office to discover the latest goodies I had hoarded there. They helped me eat the candy, although I drank the beer by myself. They understand that their daddy studies holidays, and they contribute items of interest to me on a regular basis. So to Hannah, Will, and Ian, my love and thanks for everything. Of course, Lucy Long has been the most patient, understanding, and helpful person I know. She has learned to explain her husband's eccentricities to friends without missing a beat, and she is my partner in the fullest sense. My thanks to her for allowing me to do my work. Without my family I am sure I would be helpless. The same is true for my friends, my colleagues in the department of Popular Culture at Bowling Green State University, and my students. My sincere thanks to them all.

Introduction

For many years I have been researching, writing about, and enjoying holiday celebrations in the United States and abroad. Recently I have become specifically interested in the many ways holidays are manifested in commercial products and the mass media. As part of this ongoing interest, in 1994 I offered a course entitled Holidays and Popular Culture at Bowling Green State University. As one assignment, I had each student choose a mass-marketed commercial holiday product and attempt to contact someone at the company who could speak responsibly about it. Students wrote to and telephoned, with varying degrees of success, greeting card designers, candy company executives, alcoholic beverage producers, and collectibles manufacturers. One student received what I think is an interesting and somewhat revealing response. She questioned the design of an Easter card. The response came from the senior creative developer of a major card manufacturer, who wrote that the designer of the card in question was no longer working for the company, but went on to say that "the decision-making process for greeting card product/subject matter is driven by a number of different factors: consumer preference, product analysis, retail testing, marketing decisions, as well as the seasonal symbolism appropriate to the occasion. I think this type of analysis will prove frustrating to someone outside our industry who is seeking intellectual rationalization for aesthetic choices, when the choices are more clearly linked to business and commercial considerations."

I find this interesting because the respondent assumes that individuals operate outside of culture, and that categories of intellect, aesthetics, business, and commerce are discrete and even unrelated. On the contrary, I would suggest that they are intimately linked. In fact, it can be argued persuasively that they are transformations of each other. Certainly, in the popular market, this is true of aesthetics and economics. Nowhere is this more evident than in the area of holidays, where people regularly decry the commercialization of what are felt to be sacred (or at least sacrosanct) occasions. The commercialization is felt to be a violation, a profaning of the sacred character of these special times. However, recent works by Waits (1993), Miller (1993), and Schmidt (1995) have explored the relationships among commerce, materialism, and the altruism of Christmas, and these suggest not only that there might be a necessity for the existence of commercialism at Christmas; they also explore how these apparent conflicts are resolved.

"New" Christmas tins from Great Britain, 1895. Products tied into the holidays have long been a feature of commercial, industrial societies.

Like all cultural expression, Christmas and other holidays are both paradigmatic and syntagmatic: that is, they are generally known and widely celebrated, but always under particular circumstances, at particular places, with a particular group. In one sense, all celebrations of a holiday are the "same," because the occasion and frequently the symbolic components are socially and historically derived. In another way, no two celebrations are ever the same. Holidays are always manifested as particular instances, particular events.

Related to this is the idea that holidays are realized only through their manifestations, and that these manifestations include material objects along with the actions, events, and behaviors associated with the particular event. An artifact that is in some way associated with a holiday, whether it be a song or a box of cereal, can be seen both as a manifestation of that social occasion and an interpretation of it. I take this insight from a popular Christmas album of 1993 by Boyz II Men. They are an Afri-

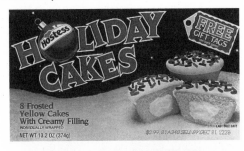

From the 1990s, holiday snack cakes for all around the year.

can American recording group who specialize in a kind of gospel-inspired harmony singing frequently referred to as 1990s-style doo-wop, a reference to a popular 1950s style. The group had the most popular Christmas album of the 1993 season, entitled *Christmas Interpretations*. Most of the songs were new and written by members of the group, and sung in their unique vocal style. In the notes accompanying the recording, the group thanks "the entire Motown family for supporting our interpretation of Christmas." I realized upon reading this and listening to the album that Christmas collections in all musical styles, including rock, country, rap, punk, and so forth, are all interpretations of Christmas. In some cases the styles of music are felt to be compatible with, or even reinforcing of, the themes generally associated with the holiday (e.g., country music), while in others, such as rap or punk, the style contrasts with the themes of the day and derives an aesthetic tension from the clash. On the other hand, other holidays, such as Halloween, are more likely to be interpreted in some of the more inversive musical styles such as punk or heavy metal because of the themes and customs associated with that holiday.

It is the purpose of this book to suggest the many, apparently infinite, interpretations, not just of Christmas, but of all holidays as manifested in popular commercial culture; to suggest that there is a cultural logic to them; and by delineating some examples, to begin to outline some of the principles and processes involved in this cultural logic. This will be done through a combination of examples and case studies. The chapters are arranged according to the processes and principles involved, with an emphasis in each chapter on at least one particular medium (e.g. print, film), genre (e.g., popular song), season (summer), or holiday. The chapters are at times impressionistic, at other times ethnographic, and sometimes speculative. The purpose is to draw attention to a sizable body of materials that might otherwise pass unnoticed, and to suggest potential readings and meanings (and importance) in them beyond what lies on the surface.

Chapter 1

Holidays and
Popular Culture

Holidays relate to the popular media, and other popular forms of cultural expression, in several ways. We will examine the uses of holidays in a variety of media: film, television, and print, including magazines, comics, and popular fiction. In television, for example, we can note the following kinds of presentations: First are specials for a holiday without a theme specifically related to that holiday. A broadcast of a movie on television such as *The Wizard of Oz* might be seen as appropriate at Christmastime, because it is a children's fantasy, for instance, but other films such as *Gone with the Wind* are also shown. Other specials are created for television exclusively and broadcast as special holiday presentations, but are not actually "about" the particular holiday in its subject matter. A second category encompasses those specials *with* a holiday theme, such as the *Bob Hope Christmas Special.* Third, regular episodes of ongoing series are frequently presented as holiday specials. You often find an episode repeated annually, such as the Christmas episodes of *I Remember Mama* in the 1950s, *Happy Days* in the 1970s, or Halloween episodes of *The Simpsons* in the 1990s.

Further, a holiday can be used more as an element of plot for dramatic and metaphorical purposes, such as the episode of *thirtysomething* that dealt with a clash of cultural traditions between the central couple in December:

he wanted a Hanukkah menorah and felt overwhelmed by Christmas. *M.A.S.H.* had a Halloween episode in which an apparently dead patient returns to life; *Northern Exposure*'s Thanksgiving episode concerned a Day of the Dead celebration and harvest feast by the Native American inhabitants of an Alaskan town. While no such celebration exists in reality (the Hispanic Days of the Dead are November 1 and 2), the show is sensitively written and filmed, and avails itself of themes appropriate to both celebrations.

Sometimes holidays are used as a plot element and also to suggest the passage of "real" time. For instance, *St. Elsewhere,* a 1980s program that was innovative in many ways, indicated that time on the show passed at the same rate as it did for the viewers by referring to holidays. One season there was an episode that was about Thanksgiving (a turkey-carving contest). On the following episode, as characters interacted in the corridors of the hospital in which the show was set, we saw workmen in the background installing a Christmas tree and putting up decorations. A Christmas episode followed, one that reflected religious imagery and other customs of Christmas. It dealt with the failure of one of the characters to have reconciled himself with his now-deceased son; although he has a Christmas party and offers fellowship to his guests by means of the wassail bowl, he cannot bring himself to attend church services to celebrate the birth of a sacred son. Instead, he stands outside the church at midnight, crying in a snowstorm. In the first episode of the new year, workmen in the background take down decorations and carry the tree away. While some of the programs in this sequence were specifically about certain holidays, and referenced appropriate themes and customs, others simply used visual references to holiday activities to index the passage of time through a season.

Similar relationships to the holidays are found in films. For instance, certain films are released at festive times of the year: John Izod, in his book *Hollywood and the Box Office 1895–1986,* says, "There has been for some time a strong seasonal weighting in cinema attendance. As the majors [large film companies] know, the peak peri-

ods fall in the Christmas and summer holidays, with Easter break a
little less busy" (1988, 182; see also A. D. Murphy, cited by Docherty,
Morrison, and Tracy 1986, 82.) Thus, many films are considered
Christmas films or summer films without actually being concerned
with those periods in their narratives. Instead they are associated
with these periods economically, and are named for the time of their
release. Other movies are basically celebrations of certain holidays:
e.g., *Easter Parade* in 1948 and *Santa Claus: The Movie* in 1985 are two
examples. Although sequels are increasingly frequent, most films are
not episodic. However, many films use holiday imagery for dramatic
purposes, as a plot element, without being considered a holiday film,
such as 1993's *The Fugitive,* wherein the fleeing escaped convict dons a
green derby and hides among the marchers in the Chicago St.
Patrick's Day parade.

The parallels between the uses of holiday motifs in film and television, while not exact, are close. The same is true of the other media
and genres we mentioned. We can identify several ways narrative
genres use holidays. Narrative forms can be especially *for* a holiday, a
set of holidays, or a season: an Easter special, for example; *about* a
holiday: a regular season episode with a holiday theme, for instance;
relevant to a holiday in a general way while not specifically about it,
such as the movie *Love Story,* which might be broadcast at Valentine's
Day, or a monster movie at Halloween, or a biblical epic at Easter; or
appropriate for a holiday, such as a movie that is considered special in
some way, such as *The Wizard of Oz* and so is appropriate for a special occasion such as Christmas or Easter. Further, holidays are used
to enhance the narratives by providing settings, themes, and symbols
that are used as plot elements for the purpose of storytelling. We will
examine these ideas at greater length throughout this book.

We will also note the principle of borrowing symbols and customs
from one holiday and applying them to another, as with holiday-
themed stalker films, and also with seasonal flags, and in the creation
of candies such as candy corn or candy canes for other seasons of the
year. Finally, I will suggest that these principles can be extended to

R. F. Outcault's Buster
Brown and friends
have their own name
for autumn. This
advertisement for a
bank in 1910
associates seasonal
symbolism with
capitalism.

include non-narrative forms such as snack foods. In this case, we see the periodization or serialization of mass cultural products that are not themselves periodical or temporally sequential in nature.

Underlying this, of course, is the larger relationship of holidays to capitalist culture and consumerism. Most of the examples used above are related to Christmas, because this holiday marks the most important period of economic activity of the year. Holidays in the United States are now and have been for at least a century intricately tied into the consumerist nature of this society. Films are released at Christmas and other special times of the year to maximize their chances of success at the box office and therefore, profits. Holiday television programming is designed to expose viewers to advertisements for commercial products, and many commercial products are especially packaged for holiday sales. The contemporary American calendar of seasonal changes and official holidays is very much a function of industrial commerce rather than agrarian time. Our holidays both reflect and support consumer industries within a capitalist political system, and as a result, we often feel that these celebrations have become too commercialized. However, one must reconcile one's feelings about holiday commercialization with one's attitudes toward contemporary American society in general. We cannot live in a money-based, profit-

driven society and expect our major ritual occasions not to reflect that society (see, for example, Belk 1993).

Christmas in July

On the cover of a 1992 catalog Santa reclines in a chaise lounge. Although he is wearing short sleeves and his pants extend only to his
kneecaps, he is instantly identifiable. Not only is the great white beard
a giveaway, but his trunks are red, with some green and white, and
holly and poinsettias are the pattern on the shirt. The catalog arrived
in early July. "Shop Early for Holiday Gift Giving," it advises. It is not
the first catalog I have received that is at least in part devoted to
Christmas; in June one arrived in the mail offering Halloween, Thanksgiving, and Christmas items. The summer Santa catalog reveals its seasonal schizophrenia in its interior pages, where red, white, and blue
products bearing the stars and stripes are offered "just in time for the
election year."

Recently, while listening to a radio station based in Windsor,
Ontario, but directed at American audiences (claiming to serve "De-
troit-Windsor,") I heard a disc jockey talking about an upcoming
week-long radio promotion, from June 30 to July 5. She referred to it
as the Festival in July. Apparently speaking spontaneously, she said,
"You know, like Christmas in July? This is the Festival in July." July
Fourth is the American celebration of Independence Day, while July 1
is Canada Day, which is celebrated, like the Fourth of July, with fireworks displays and conspicuous patriotism. It seemed to me that
these were the occasions that served at the least as an underpinning
for the radio station's promotion. I found it curious that the radio
personality equated the concept of festival in July with the large winter festival that takes place almost directly across the year rather than
with more immediate summer celebrations that actually took place
during the week of the promotion. Perhaps because the station is in
fact Canadian, and Canada Day is somewhat less important in the Canadian calendar than the Fourth of July is in the United States, where
it is a major seasonal holiday, the disc jockey's mind went first to
Christmas when advertising the station's "Festival in July." A curious

inversion indeed, flipping from the primary celebration of summer to the primary celebration of winter, but holidays, festivals, and commercial promotions may be linked together more closely today than even the more jaded observers may realize.

On the other hand, the ancient Celtic festival day of Lammas, August 1, which marked the transition from the summer to the harvest season, was sometimes called the Yule of August. As a major warm-weather festival it was compared to the major midwinter festival. Sometimes it seems as if there is nothing new under the summer or winter solstice sun; that even the most contemporary and commercial events encapsulate age-old processes and dynamics. Of course, it only seems this way: ancient peoples would have understood the meanings of their activities very differently than we do today. For this book, in our own way, we are documenting late-twentieth-century folk, popular, mass, and commercial culture associated with celebrations, including ritual, festival, ceremony, and holidays.

The same summer that I received the Christmas in July catalog, I saw a Halloween display in a department store on August 12. This is the earliest I'd ever seen Halloween products on sale, weeks before Labor Day. Since the 1980s, department stores have begun decorating for Halloween and featuring Halloween items for sale earlier and earlier. This is a testament to the increasing popularity of the day and its increasingly Christmas-like economic draw and power. Related to this is the fact that department stores have begun to display Christmas materials in October, no longer content with waiting until the Thanksgiving weekend to initiate the Christmas shopping season. Christmas is pushed forward to October, so Halloween gets bumped up to August. In a period of economic recession, Christmas commerce is even more crucial to the financial health of many businesses. And so it goes through the year: one year, on December 26, I was visiting a family member who lives far away from me. I stopped into a major department store chain to pick up a Christmas card to include with the gift I brought. I expected to find a few leftover cards, but instead I was greeted with a sea of red hearts. The card racks were filled with valentines on the day after Christmas.

Many people dislike this acceleration of seasonal time, this rushing of the seasons. Whenever I mention my interests in contemporary holiday celebrations, people frequently offer the opinion that holidays are simply excuses to get drunk, or tacky exercises in commercialism foisted upon the public by greeting card companies and other self-interested industries. However, I think there is more to the ongoing celebrations of Christmas, the New Year, Valentine's Day, St. Patrick's Day, Easter, the Fourth of July, Halloween, Thanksgiving, Hanukkah, Kwanzaa, and many others, than simply corporate greed, although that quality is certainly apparent. Indeed, it is the very popularity of these holidays that forms the basis for the ever-expanding commercialism that surrounds them. Although some so-called holidays or special occasions have in fact been invented entirely by the commercial greeting card industry, such as Boss's Day, Secretary's Day, or Grandparents' Day, the holidays I have referred to above are all either ancient festivals whose customs, symbols, and meanings are still relevant today, or they are closely related to such festivals.

Thanksgiving, for instance, is an American historical commemoration with many political overtones. Moreover, the day was not established as a national holiday until 1863 by decree of President Abraham Lincoln. Nevertheless, it takes as its model British and other European harvest feasts. It served as an important winter festival in the early colonies, substituting in New England for Christmas, which had been banned by the Puritans and was not celebrated.

In my family, our "festival in July" begins sometime prior to July 17, our eldest child's birthday. It includes August 1, my birthday, and extends to August 8, our wedding anniversary. At some time during this period, my family is usually vacationing and visiting relatives in the mountains of North Carolina and New Hampshire. As a result, our son Ian may end up having three birthday celebrations, possibly none of them actually on his birthday. The three dates are important family celebrations that together create an extended period of festivities, sometimes occurring during vacations, which are themselves a different kind of "time out of time" (see Fallasi 1987).

My family is not unique in this regard. Socially and commercially too, the calendar is flexible in real life. Many families and many individuals have their own personal calendar of special days and celebrations. People frequently adapt the stuff of the mass market to their own needs, vernacularizing and personalizing widely disseminated ideas and materials in creative ways. I have referred elsewhere to an occasion when I saw a window decoration of Christmas tinsel in the shape of the American Sign Language symbol for "I love you." I also have written about people who purposely and playfully invert traditional holiday symbolism in the neighborhood where I live, decorating plaster-of-paris chickens and displaying plastic snowmen out of season to carry holiday greetings (Santino 1994). John Fiske would term such actions resistance (Fiske 1989). On the other hand, most commercial holiday adaptations reinforce the dominant order, and are thus hegemonic.

Left: Holiday Vacuum Freshener from the 1980s. Sometimes the connection between the commercial product and the holiday is tenuous. The freshener is pine-scented, so it can be called a "Christmas tree" aroma. *Right:* St. Patrick's Day is a religious and ethnic festival that has become a national celebration. As such it is open to the same commercialism as other nationally celebrated holidays, as this 1988 photograph illustrates.

Special Christmas packages of Kleenex or Dog Bone Dog Biscuits, for instance, are produced to maximize sales and profits. Even smaller-scale, less official commercial adaptations frequently are done, at least in part, to facilitate business. For instance, a bar in Ocean City, Maryland, celebrates the end of the summer season, Labor Day weekend, as St. Patrick's Day. Appropriate decorations are displayed, customers wear green party hats, and a band performs Irish and Irish American music. St. Patrick's Day, regularly celebrated near the spring equinox, is a holiday marked by a great deal of public drinking and other behaviors that are usually frowned upon. Possibly St. Patrick's Day functions as a spring festival in the contemporary United States, with its emphasis on the color green, its icon of the shamrock plant, and its outdoor, carnivalesque excess frequently associated with celebrations of fertility (see, for instance, Stam 1988). Although it is ethnically Irish and religiously Christian, the celebration is open to anyone and attracts people of all backgrounds. "Everyone is Irish on St. Patrick's Day" say the buttons and bumper stickers. Unlike Easter, which, while clearly a celebration of the spring, is very much a religious event, St. Patrick's Day has become a national secular celebration. It bears a relationship to Easter similar to the relationship of Halloween to Christmas: an opportunity for licentious public peer-oriented festivities prior to a more solemn and specifically religious celebration among family.

The bar in the resort town of Ocean City borrowed this holiday, as it were, from its usual place on the calendar and used it to celebrate the ending of a period of temporary community among summer residents. Since St. Patrick's Day customarily features the consumption of alcohol as chief among its traditions, it is perfectly suited for the purpose.

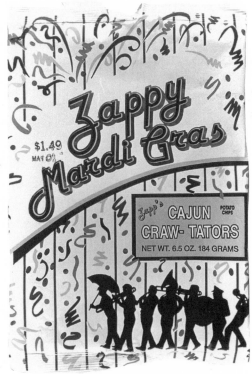

Mardi Gras is celebrated primarily in Louisiana and Alabama and has resulted in a regional popular culture that includes these potato chips packaged especially for the occasion. 1995.

More recently, and in keeping with the festival in the summer theme, an Ohio bar in which I celebrated St. Patrick's Day in March 1993 also had a "St. Patrick's day in July" event the following summer.

For the purposes of this book, I define *festivals* as periods of communal celebration, often centered around holidays. *Holiday* I have defined as a day or period of days set apart from everyday life to celebrate important historical and religious people or events (these would include, for instance, saints' days, Thanksgiving, Christmas, or Martin Luther King Jr.'s birthday), or to mark social transitions like the beginning of a new year or perhaps the turning of a season (see Santino 1994).

Although I include celebrations of the life cycle and of special occasions such as birthdays, graduations, and weddings as well, my primary focus is on holidays found on the calendar. In many such celebrations (but not all) excessive drinking is in fact widely practiced. However, sometimes a kind of controlled excess, or an excess within broader than usual limits, can be healthy. Further, celebrations frequently are occasions when everyday rules of behavior are temporarily suspended, and we are allowed to behave in ways that are usually not tolerated, as when people gather on the streets and drink publicly on New Year's Eve and Saint Patrick's Day. Even on Christmas, a religious commemoration associated with peace on earth and goodwill to all, we find excessive eating and drinking. Also, Christmas is linked with New Year's and its carnivalesque celebrations in what Miller refers to as a "twin-peaked festival" (1993: 6). Holidays and celebrations often have this quality of allowed excessive or licentious behavior—some more than others. Holidays offer periods of liminality, when normal time is suspended and people may behave in ways they otherwise may not. Mardi Gras in New Orleans, for example, is a perfect example of a festival in which it appears almost everyone goes mad. People in elaborate costumes parade the streets, while onlookers fight for cheap beads participants throw from passing floats. Public nudity and intoxication are common, and there is always the threat that the celebration will get carried away and become violent. Festivals such as Mardi Gras exemplify the inversive nature of some holiday celebrations.

The more recently invented occasions I referred to above, such as Secretary's Day, are usually based on relationships, familial, occupational, or otherwise, and they operate on a principle that is found in advertising: that of the created need. In these cases it may be more accurate to call it created guilt. That is, once a day has been declared to celebrate a relationship, for example, Boss's Day, an employer might feel slighted if she receives no tokens of respect such as cards or flowers. Somewhere in between these two extremes—very old celebrations such as Halloween or Valentine's Day on the one hand, and recently invented relational holidays on the other—are civic holidays like Flag Day, Veterans Day, or Presidents' Day, which commemorate people and events of more recent history.

Sometimes, such holidays develop meanings quite apart from their overt referents. The best examples of this are Memorial Day and Labor Day. Created to honor the Civil War dead, Memorial Day has expanded to include remembrances of fallen warriors from all national conflicts, and is a time when many families visit and decorate the graves of their loved ones, veterans or not. Labor Day, on the other hand, honors working people

Originally a day of remembrance for Civil War soldiers, Memorial Day has become a seasonal and commercial marker in the contemporary American calendar. 1986 advertisement.

in the United States. In addition, however, due to the dates on which they are celebrated, these days have taken on seasonal significance: Memorial Day, publicly celebrated on the last Monday in May, is widely regarded in the United States as the opening of the summer season, while Labor Day, the first Monday in September, marks its close. Because both these days are observed on Mondays, their observance creates three-day weekends. Each of these extended weekends has become a festive occasion, and it is possible that their seasonal significance as ritual markers of the opening and closing of a period that is itself a special time of the year is more important to many people than the stated themes of the holidays themselves.

This conflict of overt or manifest content with actual social use of holiday celebrations was the subject of the address I heard on Memorial Day, 1993, in Bowling Green, Ohio. The featured speaker, an army lieutenant, gave a brief history of the origins of the day, then noted that although it was begun as a commemoration of the Civil War dead, the occasion today is for many people perceived as the holiday weekend that opens the summer. He went on to say that while this was all right, we should all remember the actual message and intent of the holiday. Listening to the speaker, I was reminded of the many church sermons I have heard at Christmastime, exhorting the public to remember that Christmas is actually a religious event, the commemoration of the birth of Christ. Many holidays, including Easter and Labor Day, although they do not otherwise resemble each other (some are religious while others are civic and political) share this internal conflict. Although the history of the holiday, its primary rationale, is specific and usually commemorative of a historical, religious, or legendary event, its uses and meanings in society are determined in part by the time of year in which it occurs. As a result, representatives of institutions like the military, labor unions, or the church remind us regularly of the official meaning and purpose of these occasions.

Much of our popular culture is structured around this seasonal flow. To stay with the Memorial Day–summer–Labor Day example, for instance, it is obvious that summer calls forth all sorts of activities, including picnics, outings to the beach or mountains, car trips, air travel, and so on. Products and advertisements with a red, white, and blue motif are everywhere. Sun tan lotion, beach accessories, snack foods, and easy-light charcoal for the backyard barbecue are but a few examples. In addition, Memorial Day weekend is an important time for the movie industry. Films are released then and throughout the summer, in hopes of reaping blockbuster profits. Products that have no intrinsic seasonal qualities, such as beer, are heavily advertised for the many beach parties of the season. Ironically, the same beers and other beverages will be advertised with midwinter imagery for Christmas just a few months after the big summer push. Ultimately, holidays provide an invisible structure to the American year, incorpo-

rating many of its eth-
nic, regional, religious,
occupational, familial,
national, and interna-
tional aspects.

The different cus-
toms traditional to a
holiday dictate the ways
that holiday will be
commercialized. An
obvious example is
trick-or-treating at Hal-

Summer Pepsi and
winter Pepsi. 1993.

loween, where youngsters go from door to door asking for treats. The candy industry clearly capitalizes on this custom, forever invent-ing new ways to expand an already lucrative market. Thanksgiving, on the other hand, is one of the few holidays on the contemporary American calendar that is not geared primarily for children. All at-tempts so far to merchandise it that way with, for instance, cute stuffed turkeys have failed. Instead, the holiday tends to place the el-dest members of a family in a place of honor. The principal compo-nent of the day is the dinner meal, which often takes place at the resi-dence of the grandparents if they are living. This means that children and grandchildren must travel to this ancestral home, "over the river and through the woods, to Grandmother's house," as the well-known rhyme has it. It is perhaps significant that in Lydia Maria Child's original poem it was to "grand*father's* house we go." In many families, the senior male ceremonially carves the turkey, using special cutlery for the occasion. These customs put a decidedly masculine, patriarchal slant on the celebration. Nevertheless, the actual cooking is most often done by a woman, regardless of who ritually carves the centerpiece bird. Moreover, the turkey, stuffed, plump, capable of feeding many for many days, is a kind of symbol of bounty, of almost unending plenty, similar to the other Thanksgiving symbol, the cornucopia (and in a different way, to Santa's stuffed bag of toys). In this regard, Thanksgiving has a nurturing quality to it, a quality socially regarded as feminine. So in taking the Thanksgiving poem to heart, the American people have changed grandfather to grandmother.

Since it is on a Thursday, thus creating a four-day weekend, and since so many of us go "home," that is, to the residence of the eldest generation of the family, Thanksgiving Day weekend is the most heavily traveled period of the entire year. Vast sums of money are spent traveling at Thanksgiving, as reflected in the film *Planes, Trains, and Automobiles,* a Thanksgiving tale starring Steve Martin and John Candy. It is a story of two men trying to get home for Thanksgiving. One of the men, it turns out, is homeless, but he finds a home and surrogate family when he is invited to the other character's family Thanksgiving dinner.

Despite the fact that Thanksgiving is not a child-oriented holiday, and lacks a gift-giving tradition, it is a mistake to think it is not economically important. Money *is* spent, on travel and turkey dinners. Like all holidays, the economics are elaborated according to the customs associated with the occasion. The candy industry certainly makes more money at Halloween than at Thanksgiving, despite the boxes of chocolates we bring with us to Grandma's. And while potato chips, hot dogs, soft drinks, wine coolers, and beer are always popular, food outlets and advertisers give these a special push at Memorial Day, Independence Day, and Labor Day, when picnics are most likely to be held. During the summer, outdoor events like picnics and back-yard barbecues become the primary celebratory food events, and so plastic dishes, cups, spoons, and forks are sold for the hot dogs and hamburgers, soft drinks, and beer that are consumed (for food and festival, see Humphrey and Humphrey 1988). The holidays and the seasons have far-reaching economic consequences, and upon reflec-tion, one can see that the idea of the seasonal item transcends holiday packaging and is really quite extensive.

Calendrical festivals have always been used as markers for pastoral, agricultural, political, and economic cycles. They still are. Historically, for instance, the ancient Celtic (Irish, Scottish, and Welsh) festival of Samhain (pronounced Sahwin) on November 1, which is one likely precursor to our modern Halloween, was viewed as a day by which the cattle should all be brought into the stables from pasture and all crops harvested. Not only do such considerations still hold true in rural areas of both Ireland and the United States today (see, for in-stance, Sadler 1994), but in addition, our holidays are used to mea-sure yearly progress and passage in many areas of contemporary life: political, economic, religious, occupational, and familial. Merchants look to holiday trade (especially Christmas) as the lifeblood of their businesses; politicians exploit holidays as opportunities for public rela-tions (marching in the Saint Patrick's Day parade, for instance); enter-tainment products are released seasonally, and churches vie with the popular media to establish the primacy of their calendars, emphasizing the sacred over the secular.

An interesting example of this "clash of calendars" is found in the materials distributed by Liturgy Training Publications (LTP) in Chi-cago, which include books, calendars, weekly bulletins, and even placemats. Most of these are intended for church use; I first became aware of the company when I saw, in a local Roman Catholic church, a beautiful poster calendar of the liturgical year. The colors and design suggested a popularized version of medieval woodcuts; the colors, tapestries and stained glass. The company also publishes handouts that can be distributed along with the weekly bulletin of the parish church. These too are distinguished by what I consider very attractive designs. Additionally, they have a particular appeal to me because of my interest in holidays and conceptions of sacred and secular periods of time. The LTP materials include contemporary secular occasions in their materials as well. Their calendars reflect the contemporary American round of celebrations by including ethnic festivals like the Day of the Dead, nonreligious commemorations such as Martin Luther King Jr.'s birthday, Earth Day, and the summer solstice.

The approach taken to these nonreligious events is interesting. Usually they are incorporated somehow into a religious context; that is, they are read as having meaning that is, while not doctrinal, still important in a more general way. Martin Luther King Jr.'s sacrifices in the name of morality and freedom, for instance, have obvious relevance to Christianity. The concepts of renewal and respect for the earth, likewise, can be viewed as compatible with Christian teachings, and this is how they are presented.

The following is one example of the way secular events, in this case May Day, are related to the Roman Catholic church calendar. The text, entitled "Merry May," is from a handout distributed in church on April 25, 1993, the Third Sunday after Easter.

> This coming Saturday is May Day. It's time to hoist the maypole. Any pole will do, even a broomstick. . . . A maypole is the scepter of the maylord. He comes in to love his maylady, who arrives in a veil of flowers. All are invited to this mythical marriage, called "spring."
>
> Christians drew a parallel from this fanciful explanation of the fertile loveliness of the season. The risen Christ is the maylord. Christ's scepter is the holy cross. And the church—all the baptized—are the bride. . . Eastertime is a kind of honeymoon that can be seen even in the heavens. In late spring and early summer the moon rides low in the southern sky, not high as it does in winter. So it takes on a lovely golden cast; it becomes a "honeymoon."
>
> Remember maybaskets? They weren't much to look at—often little more than cut up egg cartons with violets poked into them.

The fun wasn't so much in making the baskets as in delivering them. On May Day you snuck a basket onto a neighbor's front stoop, rang the doorbell and then quickly hid—a pleasant prank.

May Day is Halloween in reverse. Instead of uninvited autumnal guests (and ghosts), there can be unexpected Eastertime gifts. It's no accident that the two days are six months apart. There's a balance here, and a revival of the maybasket custom in your neighborhood may just tip the scales in favor of giving instead of taking.

Typically the style of writing is popular, and the subjects addressed (May Day, maypoles, honeymoons, and Halloween) are secular. (Other than their proximity to each other, May Day and Easter are not associated in the secular calendar. In the church calendar, however, May Day falls within the forty days of Easter.) The essay contains some interesting ideas, but its purpose seems to be to subsume and reinterpret secular customs in the contexts of the Christian calendar and doctrine.

The texts of these handouts frequently address the clash of secular and sacred conceptions of time. At Christmas, the popular pattern of the holidays as a period of time that begins at Thanksgiving, peaks at Christmas, and ends with New Year's Day is challenged by pointing out that in the Roman Catholic church calendar, Christmastime begins with Christmas Day. Memories of an earlier time when trees were put up on Christ-

The sacred made secular and commercial. This ad borrows the idea of the Advent calendar for its Christmas countdown. 1988.

mas Eve rather than taken down on December 26 are nostalgically invoked, and a return to this pattern is suggested. Begin the celebration on Christmas Day for twelve days, they advise; put the tree up on Christmas Eve, and restore Advent to a sacred but somber period of anticipation. In a sense, the Liturgy Training Publications represent an attempt to popularize the sacred and to place sacred meaning on popular, secular celebrations.

Holidays, along with the celebrations of the life cycle and special occasions like sports victories or troops returning home from war, permeate every aspect of our society. Not surprisingly, then, holidays are reflected in most cultural expressions and in most social institutions. While the dogmas of organized religions form a kind of official culture, materials like those examined above are certainly popular in design and execution (though reminiscent of earlier styles), and more important, they are intended for widespread dissemination.

Popular Culture

Popular culture has been defined in many different ways. Perhaps the broadest conception refers to the entire way of life of a definable or boundaried group of people, small or large. We would include then, under this definition, Americans, New Englanders, Cajuns, or New Yorkers, as some examples. Used this way, the term can be used to refer to, but is not restricted to, either large groups or smaller subgroups within society. Popular culture is also used to refer to the products of the mass media, as well as any other items widely disseminated throughout a society. Used this way, popular culture applies most generally to media such as film, video, and print, and would include genres like westerns, superhero comics, soap operas, greeting cards, newspapers, country music, and so on. Other widely disseminated manifestations of popular culture may lie at least partly outside the mass media. Thus we see items like beer cans, toilet paper, and even bank certificates of deposit being linked with holidays. While a great deal of this material is ephemeral, that does not make it any less important. As in the example above of the church-distributed sacred calendar, people are involved in many institutions in society, including organized religion, education, businesses, and government at all levels. As Americans we can be assumed to have a general knowledge of at least some aspects of these. While together these institutions form the basis of our official culture, they also provide the basis of a broad popular culture.

Finally, popular culture refers, not simply to the mass media, but to the popular uses of the mass media. This formulation implies an ethnographic dimension to the study of popular culture. People go to movies, watch television, and read novels, but which people choose which products, and under what circumstances? What meanings and values do they derive from them? Are people really passive consumers, manipulated by advertising, or is the process more dynamic than this? We can view contemporary holiday celebrations as popular cultural events themselves, which are made up of other popular aspects such as foodways, music, dance, games, and so on. Further, some of the ways people celebrate holidays have to do with personal use of mass media products: playing *The Temptations' Christmas Card* (1969) as a way of opening the Christmas season; reading Dickens's *A Christmas Carol* on Christmas Eve; going to a production of *The Nutcracker,* or simply going to a movie during the holidays. Holidays and popular culture interrelate in a variety of often complex ways.

The value of holidays is sometimes dismissed. "Any excuse to have a party," people say to me. However, this does not explain why certain activities take place on certain occasions and not others. Why, for instance, do people take to the

Holiday Lucky Charms. There seems to be no clear connection between breakfast cereal and Christmas, but many companies now issue holiday packaging in December. 1994.

streets on Halloween and New Year's Eve, but not Thanksgiving or Christmas? Why do people celebrate on some occasions and not others, and why do those celebrations take the shapes they do? Americans celebrate in many different ways, and the variety of these activities is reflected in the artifacts, the things, of our popular culture. These are far too numerous to attempt an exhaustive list. This book, then, is selective in nature, but broad-ranging enough to suggest the range of popular materials that are holiday-related in one way or another, and to indicate the many ways in which holidays are of great significance to our society. We will examine holiday-themed products like films and television programs, along with holiday-oriented commercial products like beer and breakfast cereal. We will also look at seasonally related patterns of behavior. Finally, we will explore the relationships between the ways people celebrate seasonal festivals and holidays and the many official institutions that may or may not sponsor them. These include both church and state, but in the United States, it is commercial industry that has capitalized most on the various aspects of traditional celebrations. Significant numbers of Americans travel at Thanksgiving, give away candy at Halloween, exchange gifts at Christmas, drink champagne on New Year's Eve, and send flowers on Valentine's Day. All of these activities generate enormous sums of money. Our holiday celebrations are very much a part of the national economy.

Mythic Salesmen

Shopping malls these days feature trick-or-treating at Halloween. Kids go from store to store and receive sweets and coupons good for the merchandise the store sells. A memo dated October 25, 1990, that was distributed to employees of a chain of record stores in Ohio neatly illustrates the commercial and capitalistic exploitation of traditional holidays, in this case Halloween. Actually, it shows the way specific traditional customs are manipulated. On the surface, it would appear that a store is giving away something for free, or at least making a nice gesture to the public. However, the memo reveals that the trick-or-treating is viewed entirely as a sales device (and good public relations simultaneously). The memo states:

> With Halloween approaching, we would like to do something special in our stores. By now everyone should have received some decorations for their stores. Most of the Malls have sent flyers announcing the time for Trick-or-Treating by the kids. Some of the Malls are passing out candy at their entrance and exits.
>
> We would like the [store's name] employees to pass out candy in their stores on that afternoon or evening. Candy has been purchased in bulk and will be sent to each store from the warehouse. We also had coupons printed up for $1.00 off any CD in the store. These are to be passed out along with the candy, and any extra coupons should be used as bag stuffers. The expiration date on the coupon is Nov. 1.
>
> In the spirit of Halloween, we would like to encourage employees working when candy is being passed out to wear some sort of costume or mask.
>
> Thanks for your participation, and have fun!

PLEASE BE ADVISED THAT COUPONS ARE NOT TO BE PLACED ON THE COUNTER BY THE CHECKOUT. THESE COUPONS ARE SUPPOSED TO BRING IN ADDITIONAL CUSTOMERS TO INCREASE YOUR SALES. IF YOU HAND THEM OUT AT THE CHECKOUT TO A CUSTOMER WHO WAS

This ad exploits the connection between the symbolism used by the rock band the Grateful Dead and the returning dead of Halloween. 1989.

GOING TO BUY A CD ANYWAY, YOU ARE DEFEATING THEIR PURPOSE.
PLEASE RETURN REDEEMED COUPONS WITH YOUR WEEKLY SALES
SUMMARY.

*If you feel it would be more helpful to your store to start passing out the coupons in store bags this weekend, please do so.

That is the memo in its entirety. The sections in capital letters were printed that way in the original. The point: do not distribute these giveaways to just anybody; use them (and the holiday custom of trick-or-treating) to lure new customers into the shop. Mall trick-or-treating creates the impression that the shops are merely participating in the fun of the community and offering a bargain as well, but the reality is somewhat less altruistic than that.

Capitalism is more than the economic system of the United States; it is the basis for its culture. Like any cultural system, we who are immersed in it, we who in our actions recreate it constantly, cannot see it. Most of us are unaware of the ways our social values and behaviors validate a capitalist ethos. Only when these activities are exaggerated during festival periods are they recognized, and usually condemned as crass. Still, even a cursory examination of holidays and popular culture reveals capitalism and commercialism at almost every turn. The holidays are used to sell merchandise (see, for instance, Schmidt 1991; Waits 1993; Miller 1993). Not only are holidays created and elaborated for commercial purposes, and not only are holiday symbols

related to commercial products, but even the historical, legendary, and mythic figures that in reality belong to us all are seen endorsing various goods. Our capitalist Santa Claus holds a bottle of Coke in his hand. In a summer advertising campaign, the sun

Santa drinks a Coke;
Santa drinks a Pepsi.
1993.

itself drinks a Coke! George Washington shops for a certain brand of cherry pie, and Benjamin Franklin uses a particular bank.

There is simply no way to discuss holiday celebrations in the United States today without getting into the issue of commercialization. In his book on Christmas gift-giving, William Waits mentions that the word *commercialization,* as applied to Christmas (and by extension to other calendrical celebrations), is used in at least five different ways. Does the word mean, he asks, "that there was an increase in the use of money in connection with the celebration, that there were larger sales volumes, that there was more promoting of sales at Christmas, that buying and selling came to assume a larger role in the celebration of the holiday, or that the celebration was related to a surrounding consumption culture? All of these developments—and more—tend to get subsumed under the label of 'commercialization'" (1993, 2–3).

For this reason, Waits chooses not to use the term, although he does deal with the issues. I do use the term, recognizing that it is frequently used by people to describe what they feel is wrong with contemporary holiday celebrations. Again, any reasonable treatment of holidays must confront the issues of commerce, and while I recognize that some readers will feel that these are the essential issues, I do not want this book to be about the commercialization of holidays exclusively, or even mostly. Most of the items mentioned throughout this book are commercial products, and many of them are frivolous. That some holidays are created to make money for card and flower companies, that television specials are designed to deliver an audience to a product, that holiday themes are exploited by publishers to sell paperback books more easily—these things are self-evident. I am interested in the many ways holidays and popular culture intersect, including, but not limited to, the above. I examine various artifacts and genres of the mass media as material, audible, and visual examples of this intersection.

We will try to determine whether certain holidays are more likely to be represented in certain media or by certain genres; which holiday customs lend themselves to exploitation by commercial industry;

and how people use and adapt folk tradition, the electronic media,
and mass culture to create meaningful personal and familial ways of
celebrating.

The New Old-Fashioned Way

Traditions, so-called, may be documented in books and encyclopedias
of calendar customs. Once a customary behavior has been recorded
as such for posterity, people sometimes feel that only such published
accounts are "real" traditions, and thus feel that their own activities
are somehow degenerate, of less value, or at worst not valid at all. In
reality, what we call tradition is the enactment of intent, usually based
on ideas that are old in society, and expressive in nature (see, for instance, Glassie 1968, 1972). Tradition is a form of human behavior.
Traditions arise from people interacting, behaving according to some
shared sense of a common script, doing certain things thought to be
appropriate under certain circumstances. Whatever its history, a living tradition is always contemporary, enacted in the present, even if
nostalgia sometimes plays a role. As such, traditions are always being
reinvented, if not actually invented for the first time. The title of this
book reflects the concept of the "invented tradition" (Hobsbawm and
Ranger 1983), and refers to the idea that an "old-fashioned" custom
may in fact be a recent cultural emergence.

The reinvention of Christmas in the Victorian era is one example,
and the use of yellow ribbons to welcome home Americans held hos-
tage in Iran in 1979–1980 is another (Golby and Purdue 1986; Santino
1992). While there were precedents for the use of the yellow ribbon,
the actual custom was a new one. Yellow ribbons had never been
used on a mass scale for this purpose before, and their use was
strongly influenced by the popularity of the hit song "Tie a Yellow
Ribbon 'Round the Ole Oak Tree," as sung by Tony Orlando and
Dawn. Later, during the Persian Gulf war in 1991, people again displayed yellow ribbons, and again the meanings and referents of those
ribbons had changed. Yet the tradition was thought to be an old one

in 1979 when it first emerged, much like, one suspects, the adaptation
of the German Christmas tree in Victorian England (Santino 1992).
According to Weiser, in the United States, President Benjamin
Harrison referred to the White House Christmas tree as old-
fashioned in the late nineteenth century, even though as recently as
1851 Charles Dickens had referred to Christmas trees as new German toys (Weiser 1952, 121). It is the act of decorating, the very act
of celebrating, that is old-fashioned. How we celebrate may involve
very old customs adapted and reinvented to suit contemporary society, and it may involve wholly new forms and ideas.

Holidays begin with people doing things that they recognize as relating to and deriving from a particular set of ideas that are more or
less shared in their social group. "Old-fashioned" ways are always being made new; if they were not, they would die. New ways of celebrating, of imagining special occasions, become "old-fashioned" in
the sense that they fit the occasion and allow people to participate in
it. So in 1958, when Brenda Lee sang Johnny Marks's *Rockin' Around
the Christmas Tree* ("Everyone dancin' merrily in the new old-fashioned way") to a rock and roll beat, she was using Christmas tradition
in a contemporary way. Now, decades later, the song and others of
its time have become Christmas standards.

Johnny Marks is also the composer of the song *Rudolph the Red-
Nosed Reindeer,* which he wrote in 1949, based on a story written by
Robert L. May as a department store giveaway. In the late 1950s,
however, rock and roll was popular, so many Christmas songs were
done in that style, like Lee's *Rockin' Around the Christmas Tree* and
Jingle Bell Rock sung by Bobby Helms. *Rockin' Around the Christmas Tree*
is performed in a mid-tempo rockabilly style. It features a prominent
electric guitar. Initially, the juxtaposition of the old and the new, the
traditional and the modern, the Christmas tree with rock and roll,
was shocking. Today, the same is true for holiday songs performed in
punk or rap musical styles. Interestingly, many (if not most) of the
punk and rap Christmas songs are quite reverent toward the values of
Christmas. Hypocrisy and crass commercialism are attacked merci-

lessly, but respect for the essential dignity of all people and the central life-affirming values of Christmas abounds.

Marks's songs are still heard at Christmas, and Rudolph has become a part of the Santa Claus mythos. Who would have thought in 1958 that *Rockin' Around the Christmas Tree* would someday be considered a Christmas classic? When Johnny Marks came up with the idea of the "new old-fashioned way," he anticipated by several decades the scholarly concept of invented traditions as set forth by Hobsbawm and Ranger (1983). Holiday traditions are continually being both invented and reinvented. Old-fashioned ways are often new. In a postindustrial society such as ours, it is reasonable to expect that these will be manifested in the mass media and in the many forms of mass culture.

Of course, holidays continue to be celebrated on the personal and small group levels. That is how holidays are enacted and made meaningful. People actively use the mass media and mass-produced artifacts to create personal rituals and symbols. It is the interaction of these levels—the personal, the small group, the popular media, and mass culture—that is of interest. One does not necessarily displace the other. However, the many ways in which holidays and popular culture are interrelated have not been closely examined. They should not be overlooked or taken for granted. This book is about the new old-fashioned ways in which many Americans go about living the holidays and seasons of their lives.

Chapter 2

The Year in Candy

Holidays and the Mass Media

No one would deny that Christmas permeates American society, although people may disagree as to whether this is a good thing. Regardless, it will come as little surprise that one can obtain a multitude of Christmas-related materials, including pencils, breakfast cereals, socks, and even toilet paper. What might come as a surprise, however, is that this same abundance of consumer goods is available for other holidays as well, such as Halloween, Valentine's Day, and St. Patrick's Day. Just as Christmas in Victorian Britain was recreated in its now familiar modern guise, other calendrical holidays are becoming elaborated and transformed in the late-twentieth-century United States. This growth in holiday-related activities is almost certainly a result of industry-sponsored efforts, but it also reflects a genuine growth in the popular participation in contemporary calendrical celebrations.

What are the interrelationships between holidays and popular culture? A nationally franchised sandwich shop advertisement depicts a Christmas tree bedecked with submarine sandwiches. Taco Bell celebrates *Cinco de Mayo* on its soft drink containers, while Corona beer issued a *Cinco de Mayo* T-shirt. Miller beer is the pot of gold at the end of the rainbow on a St. Patrick's Day poster. State lotteries tempt consumers with "Holiday Cash," "Winner

Wonderland," "Spring Fling," and "Summer Sizzlers" games. The
United States Postal Service not only issues Christmas stamps annually, but also issues "Love" stamps around Valentine's Day and "Special Occasion" stamps at other times of the year. A shopper can buy
Cap'n Crunch's Christmas Crunch, or Holiday Lucky Charms cereals
in December, Home Run Crunch in the summer, and a heart-shaped

Left: Corona, a
Mexican beer, also has
Cinco de Mayo
products and
advertising. 1990.
Right: The range of
items tied into
holidays and seasons
in our society is
extraordinary. Special
lottery tickets for
winter, spring,
summer, Father's Day,
and the Fourth of July
are available. 1989.

The U.S. Postal
Service issued this love
stamp and these Asian
New Year stamps in
February 1995.

Nestle's Crunch Spring
Series. There is also a
Winter Series with
pictures of Santa
Claus. 1994.

Nestle's Crunch bar in February ("You're Perfectly *Scrunch*ous. Won't you be my Valentine?" the rose-colored wrapper reads).

On the popular television comedy *Cheers*, Sam Malone spends Valentine's Day in an annual amorous rendezvous with a lady he sees only on that day; Judge Harry Stone relived *It's a Wonderful Life* in a special one-hour episode of *Night Court*, as did Maddie Hayes of *Moonlighting* before him in an episode entitled "It's a Wonderful Job," while on *Roseanne*, *It's a Wonderful Life* is redone for Halloween. And of course, every year Linus waits, inevitably, for the Great Pumpkin.

Popular films also feature holiday themes: *White Christmas, Miracle on 34th Street, Easter Parade,* and *Holiday Inn;* Bill Murray in *Scrooged* and *Groundhog Day;* Woody Allen's *A Midsummer Night's Sex Comedy;* the stalker films *Halloween, Friday the 13th, Prom Night, April Fool's Day,* and others; but movies are linked to the calendar in other ways as well: the two major periods of the year for the release of films to theaters are the Christmas season, which begins with Thanksgiving weekend, and summer, which begins in May with schools' closing. Good business at the box office at either of these times equals major success.

Holidays, celebrations, and the seasons are manifested not only in the obvious arenas of greeting cards and television specials, of children's books and Christmas songs. They are expressed in our clothing, in our food, on soft drink cans, in comic books and coffee mugs and even financial certificates of deposit. Holidays are themselves a form of popular culture, of course, but as Smith has said of festivals, they are a genre composed of other genres (1972). Each of these genres is a category of human social behavior, and each object is both the result of human behavior and intended for use in a social context. As much as we are interested in the popular material culture of holidays—the objects, foods, and decorations that help define the occasions—in the end celebrations are enactments of human behavior. Celebrations can in fact be seen as sets of behaviors. People *use* these ritual and symbolic objects. They send the cards, play the recordings, and fly the flags. Along with the songs, many of them copyrighted and played incessantly on the radio; the greeting cards and

Valentines that support an entire industry; the myriad trinkets done up in stars and stripes available in any store (especially between Memorial Day and Labor Day); the pumpkins and turkeys and champagne and eggs and matsohs and kielbasa that seem to swell the supermarkets, and the plane fares and crowds of passengers for the long trips home, are the singing, sending, saluting, and sighing after a heavy meal.

The symbolic objects, some homemade, some storebought, are tools for realizing celebrations. On a general level, celebrations are distinguished by the customary activities thought to be appropriate, such as accepting gifts and blowing out candles on a cake, or exchanging gifts and lighting electric candles placed in a window. More specifically, each enactment of a celebration—be it a birthday party or Christmas—is a unique combination of participants and activities: no two Christmases, no two birthday celebrations, are ever the same.

Holidays as commercial enterprises have a profound economic underpinning in American society. Are they simply moneymaking schemes promoted by greeting card companies, artificially vitalized by a capitalist life-support system? Some, perhaps, are. There is no question that Secretary's Day, Grandparents' Day, or Boss's Day are recent inventions of the greeting card industry. But Halloween, Valentine's Day, New Year's Day, and so many others, are not, although they also are heavily promoted and merchandised. Rather than view the enormous volume of economic activity that surrounds calendrical celebrations in this country simply as artificially inflated consumer gouging, it is just as reasonable to see it as evidence of the great popular importance of holidays and celebrations (see Schmidt 1995).

Holidays are economic in nature, but they are also religious, patriotic, ethnic, occupational, familial, and personal. Depending on the holiday, some emphasize some of these factors more than others. Holidays do not merely help sell things, thereby helping the economy. They *are* the economy, reflecting economic flow and flux according to the seasons. Holidays are not mere microcosms of society; they are society written large in parades, floats, masquerade costumes, house decorations, and sporting contests: dramatic, larger-than-life gestures that speak of deep social and cultural issues.

Holidays and any one form of popular culture interact in more ways than one. Even the most commercialized aspects of holidays reflect various population groups. Far from being a monolithic leveler of culture, perhaps even in spite of industry efforts to render them just that, events such as holidays, life-cycle rites of passage, and seasonal celebrations doggedly reflect a cultural pluralism. This is particularly evident when various popular forms are compared with each other: that is, the year as manifested in candy, so to speak, is different from the year as manifested in comics, or popular music.

The Year in Candy

M&Ms produces a candy product called Holidays. These are standard M&Ms, except that the candies included in the packages are restricted to colors appropriate to the particular holiday in question. Likewise, the packages themselves announce the holiday they are meant for as much by color symbolism as by the use of the standard iconography of particular celebrations. For instance, the first time I ever saw these candies was in the spring of 1986. Two varieties were available in the store: plain and peanut. The plain were in a yellow bag, the peanut in pink. Both packages depicted pastel-colored M&Ms within, and a drawing of a small rabbit with an Easter basket. This drawing clearly specified the candy as intended for Easter, but the pastel colors of the bags communicated their relevance to spring generally and Easter in particular from across the shopping aisle.

The following December, not surprisingly, Holidays were available again, in a red package for plain and green for peanut. Accordingly, the candies contained within were colored red and green. The specific Christmas iconography on the package was restricted to a wreath and a Christmas tree. Once again, for me at least, the colors of the packages carried the initial load of meaning.

I began to keep my eye out for this brand of candy. I was a little

surprised, though I should not have been, to see Holidays again in
January, again in a red package, but also with white on it, and hearts
emblazoned across it: red and white M&Ms for Valentine's Day. Easter brought back the pastel colors, with light green and light blue bags
added to the yellow and purple. The Easter line eventually increased
to include mint chocolate and almond M&Ms.

On through the next couple of years the pattern remained the
same. Holidays candy was issued for Easter, Christmas, and
Valentine's Day. The packages' design changed a bit from year to year,
but never drastically. Easter itself was never mentioned on the package, as were neither Christmas or Valentine's Day, but the packages
left no doubt as to the occasion for which the candy was targeted. I
began to wonder: why manufacture candy for these three holidays
and none others? Why weren't there any M&M Holidays for Halloween, an obvious occasion for such candy? There are several possible
reasons for this. First, candy is very much a part of Easter, Christmas,
and Valentine's Day. Since they were packaged loosely in a large bag,
these candies, color-coded for their particular holidays, were probably meant to be placed in a dish and made available for guests during
social gatherings. They could also be scattered in an Easter basket,
like jelly beans, or eaten directly from the package, of course. Generally though, the most likely use was by adults for their holiday get-
togethers. At Halloween, a person would not give out individual
M&Ms to trick-or-treaters, for several reasons, among them the cur-
rent suspicion of unwrapped candies. M&Ms manufactures a separate
product, a large package of M&Ms in small "treat-sized" bags intended
for Halloween trick-or-treating. These cover the Halloween candy
market. The company seemed to envisage that holiday as being less
conducive to adult holiday parties, with its overwhelming focus on
children, at least when it comes to candy.

Likewise, there was no Thanksgiving-oriented Holidays candy.
Thanksgiving is a holiday that is overshadowed commercially by
Christmas, but it also is one (and one of the only ones) in which children are not the primary focus of the day's customs. If anything, it is
the eldest generations of the family who receive attention at Thanks-

giving. The holiday is usually celebrated in the home of the eldest generation, the home where the middle generation grew up; while Christmas is celebrated in the home of the youngest generation. The meal is the central event of Thanksgiving, prepared and presented by the grandparents, who are the focus of attention. Children have their turn in December, when Santa Claus visits their homes and leaves gifts for them. Significantly, the religious symbol of Christmas is a sacred baby, usually surrounded by doting adults, reflective of the nuclear family and the attention paid to children on this day. Thanksgiving symbolism is focused on past generations (the pilgrims, the eldest generations of "Americans"; our grandparents, the eldest generation of our family), while Christmas is focused on future generations.

With this in mind, I was interested to see in 1990 that finally a Holidays product was issued in the autumn. Two bags were available, one orange (plain) and one brown (peanut). The bags had small pumpkins—not jack-o'-lanterns—on them. "For your Fall festivities" the package proclaimed. The M&Ms inside were "in autumn colors," and the candy was on sale through November. That is to say: when M&Ms finally issued a product coinciding with Halloween and Thanksgiving, they made them generally relevant to the season but not specific to either of the two chief celebrations of that season. Pumpkins are generally symbolic of both Halloween and Thanksgiving, but no jack-o'-lanterns, black cats, turkeys, or pilgrims were to be found. The symbolism employed was that of the season (leaves) and the harvest (wheat). As such they were relevant to both holidays without being restricted to either of them.

Since the first time I saw the Holidays candy, I have noticed other candy packaged for holidays in new ways. Some of these others include "bite-sized" Milky Ways and Snickers in pastel wrappers in the spring,

Gummi Shamrocks. Many different candies are based on holiday symbols. 1992.

and in red and green wrappers in December. Nestles makes a Merry Morsels product, which are chocolate chips with colored sprinkles for baking cookies. There are many, many other candy products for various holidays, such as Gummi Shamrocks on St. Patrick's Day, or candy hearts that come in a miniature mailbox around Valentine's Day. Of all of these, however, only the M&M product actually calls itself Holidays and is available periodically. The appearance of the product maps out a sequence of significant holidays and seasons: Easter, autumn, Christmas, and Valentine's Day. Clearly, the choices of these particular holidays and season represent some corporate thinking as to which holidays can support such a product, and which cannot. There are no green and white Holidays M&Ms for St. Patrick's Day, for instance. Until 1991, there was no Holidays product for the summer, but in that year red and blue packages of Holidays offered candies colored red, white, and blue.

Contrast this year in candy to advertising campaigns and packaging for beer. There are Winter Lagers and Coors Winterfest in December, along with Christmas graphics on six- and twelve-pack containers. Rolling Rock in 1992 had a "Jingle Bell Rock" graphic. The beer industry, however, unlike any of the other products we have looked at, exploits the Super Bowl shortly after Christmas. Packaging and point of purchase displays depict television-centered parties. Other prepared foods do so too. Submarine sandwiches, chips, and pizza are heavily marketed as the appropriate party foods for the Super Bowl. It seems fitting that the Super Bowl football game, which has spawned the rise of a new, unofficial American festive event, Super Sunday, with festive gatherings of people to watch the game, is a media-oriented and media-derived event. It has been essentially created by the television networks and National Football League, and it serves their interests. Interestingly, the foods customarily eaten at these "Super Parties" are not homemade, but storebought, commercial items, just as the event is a mass-media venture promoted initially by commercial concerns. In short, if we consider food as a component of celebration, the media-created festive event is marked by commercially prepared food items.

The year in beer continues to St. Patrick's Day, for which it is heavily promoted, and then to summer as a season. Beer is heavily promoted as a component of beach life, and some beers specifically issue a summer product, such as Pete's Wicked Summer Brew or Samuel Adams Summer Wheat Brew. Then follows Halloween and autumn promotions, some featuring imagery like Elvira or a Karloffian Frankenstein's monster. Some companies claim to be "the Official Beer of Halloween." Other beers purport to have something to do with Octoberfest (which in Europe usually takes place in September). Then it is back to the myriad winter releases, such as Oldenberg Winter Ale, Coors Winterfest, or Samuel Adams Special Cranberry beer for Thanksgiving and Christmas.

The new seasonality of beer—marketed for Halloween and Octoberfest, Christmas and Winterfest, the Super Bowl, St. Patrick's Day and the summer— is not associated with the agrarian cycle. Traditionally, seasonal beers like Octoberfest and wines like Beaujolais are tied to the growth and harvest cycle underlying the processes of fermentation and brewing. Bock beer, for instance, is so named because it is brewed in late winter/ early spring, the birthing season for goats. The word *bock* is derived from the German word for goat, and many bock beers depict a goat on the bottle label. In fact, one European beer is called Celebrator. The label shows an image of a goat along with the imagery of the spring carnivals traditionally held at this time in much of Europe, and

The new seasonality of beer. 1993.

Left: Comics with
holiday themes were
sometimes issued as
special issues, and
sometimes as regular
issues within a series,
like this 1940s *Raggedy
Ann and Andy*.
Right: Christmas cover
on *Looney Tunes*. Note
the wilder, zanier
appearance of this
early version of Bugs
Bunny.

This *Little People*
comic from 1956 is
unusual in that it
depicts Thanksgiving
symbolism along with
Christmas symbolism.
The interior story also
moves from a harvest
Thanksgiving feast in
late autumn to the
arrival of Santa.

connects these with the alcoholic beverages people enjoy at
these festivals.

What we see in the cases of
these popular foodstuffs is the
creation of novelty by the introduction of serialization. The
Holidays candies are the best
examples, but one sees a similar
phenomenon with specific beer
companies: Coors Winterfest,
followed by the Super Bowl advertising, followed by St.
Patrick's Day, summer, and in time, by Halloween symbols. Recent
promotional materials for Coors include a beer for every season:
Winterfest, Eisbock, "brewed in celebration of the Spring," a wheat
beer for summer, and Octoberfest. Other advertising campaigns tie
into Memorial Day auto races along with winter and summer sports.
The summer-related advertising attempts to relate beer to the season, by presenting it as an associated component of the seasonal celebrations such as picnics, barbecues, and clambakes. So this company

uses holidays, special occasions, and the seasons every step of the way, both by issuing special seasonal products and by relating its beer to the calendar through its advertising.

Compare the years in candy and beer, as outlined above, with the year as reflected in another mass medium, comic books. Traditionally, children were the primary audience for comic books. Seasonal comics have long been a staple of the industry, generally appearing as twenty-five-cent annuals and specials, back when regular series issues cost ten cents. A look at the seasonal comics of the 1930s, '40s, and '50s reveals the following patterns: The primary special issues were for Christmas or, in some cases, winter, along with summer vacation, back-to-school, and Halloween. Little Lulu was featured annually in a Halloween special; Bugs Bunny in a Christmas special; Archie and the gang hung up their *Christmas Stocking* every year; Tom and Jerry had *Winter Fun* and *Winter Carnival* issues; Woody Woodpecker went to the *County Fair* and then *Back to School.* In addition, regular issues, as opposed to annuals and specials, also had stories for those holidays and special events. Occasionally there were New Year's stories, and more rarely, Valentine's Day. The 1940s saw titles like *Easter with Mother Goose, Christmas with Mother Goose, Santa Claus Funnies,* and *Santa Claus Parade,* but these faded in the 1950s. In 1976 Dennis the Menace was featured in a bicentennial special, and the character was also featured in some Fourth of July comics. These too were unusual, in that other characters were not featured in stories built around the Fourth of July with any regularity, although many characters had more general summer specials. In the main, the year as manifested in comics in the mid–twentieth century was the children's year: summer vacation, back-to-school (a major rite of passage for a child), Halloween, and Christmas.

Comics aren't exclusively for kids anymore, if they ever were, and the year as manifested in contemporary comics reflects the changing times and the more mature clientele. Today there are Earth Day specials, at least one parodistic St. Paddy's Day special, erotic Valentine's Day comics, and a Super Bowl special. Halloween and Christmas are both still well represented, but Halloween comics especially are far more adult in content and graphic style. More than other holidays, Halloween can support several genres of comic book publications. That is, there continue to be Halloween comics featuring "funny animals" which are targeted primarily at children, such as Donald Duck or Whacky Squirrel. However, the imagery associated with Halloween easily supports, and suggests, graphically explicit horror comics as well. As early as the 1950s, EC Comics exploited this thematic opportunity with a series of horror comics featuring ghoulish beheadings, dismemberment, and ax murders. Today's Halloween comics also include garish horror titles (none done as well as the old EC titles, however), superheroes (for instance, Captain America, in "Trick or Treat!"), and even a comic fully devoted to a fanciful retelling of the origin of Halloween, titled *All Hallows' Eve.*

Through the earlier decades, Walt Disney's characters were featured in most of the types described above. There was an annual summer *Vacation Parade,* an annual *Huey, Dewey, and Louie Back to School* special, and, every year, *Walt Disney's Christmas Parade.* In 1990,

Disney Comics began publishing four seasonal titles annually: *Spring Fever, Summer Fun, Autumn Adventures,* and *Holiday Parade.* The last is for all intents and purposes a Christmas comic, but significantly, increasing sensitivity to cultural pluralism in the United States has dictated a change in the title. The other three are not named for holidays, nor do they specifically reflect the child's year. The stories

This 1955 issue of *Action Comics* is a calendar-of-holidays Superman story.

in *Autumn Adventures,* for instance, cover a three-month season, including a back-to-school story, a Halloween-oriented tale, and a Thanksgiving-themed story. These titles, with the possible exception of the *Holiday Parade,* are named for and built around seasons, rather than specific special days within those seasons.

The comics represent changing conceptions of the celebratory year over decades, and a closer look reveals alternative approaches to the various holidays within the titles. Many of today's comics, in fact, can only be termed postmodern, in that they display a self-consciousness about the conventions of their medium. For instance, *Justice League Europe* (a superhero team) had a "Back-to-School" issue. The cover depicted the title characters in a classroom, confronting a teacher the reader sees only from behind. She is wearing black fishnet stockings and a tight skirt. The drawing is as reminiscent of a heavy-metal video, such as Van Halen's "Hot for Teacher," as it is any of the innocent 1950s titles, though it clearly plays off awareness of, and nostalgia for, the latter for its effect. This comic, and others like *Elvira's House of Mystery,* trade on their audience's awareness of long-time comic book traditions to make their statement. In a monthly sequence from summer through December, *Elvira's House of Mystery*

Left: Comics are not just for kids anymore, if they ever were. In the 1940s and 50s, neither Spring Break nor the type of image on the cover of this 1995 *Lobo Spring Break* comic would have been found in comics.
Right: A 1985 Halloween comic cover.

Sometimes a comic
will do a whole series
based on the
sequence of holidays
and special calendrical
events. 1986–87.

depicted the sexy "Mistress of
the Night" in a series of cover
drawings featuring the Fourth of
July Statue of Liberty Centennial
celebration, a back-to-school
scene, Halloween, and Christmas. Each cover contrasted the
seductive, curvaceous Elvira with
the symbols and iconography of
the seasonal events. This single
title, then, did not feature only
seasonal specials (though it did
have a Christmas special in addition to the monthly comic).

Rather, it used the calendar and its celebrations as an ongoing motif
for each of its issues.

This in turn reflects a pluralism among the audience populations.
There are still Disney comics for younger children, and Archie Com-
ics issues its Christmas specials and summer specials every year.
These too reflect the changing styles, fashions, customs, and mores of

the decades, but minimally, without radically altering the characters or the types of stories one would expect to find in those titles. The mainstream superhero titles, such as the *Justice League,* have become reflexive, playing with the conventions of seasonal comics, while others, like *Batman,* have become more graphically violent and gritty. Many comics are available only in comics specialty stores. Some of these carry an "Adults Only" or "Not Intended for Children" warning.

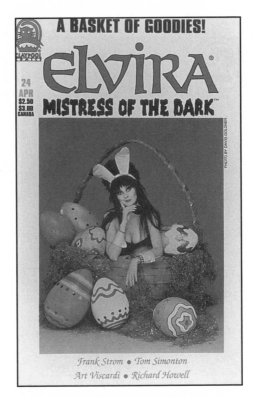

A BASKET OF GOODIES!

ELVIRA

MISTRESS OF THE DARK

24 APR $2.50 $3.00 CANADA

PHOTO BY DAVID GOLDNER

Frank Strom • Tom Simonton
Art Viscardi • Richard Howell

Another holiday-themed Elvira cover, this one from a different company. 1995.

The rise of the comic shop as an outlet for comics with a relatively small print run has been a major development that has altered and helped save the comics industry. In the past, retailers returned unsold comics to their publishers and were refunded for them. This meant that the publishers needed to print copies far in excess of what they actually sold. It also meant that the retailer had little incentive to sell, or even display the comics, because there was no risk involved. The unsold comics were simply returned. Through the 1950s and 60s, comic sales declined steadily. However, as the first few comics-only specialty stores opened in the late 1970s, they initiated a different system of distribution: the retailer paid for what was ordered in advance, with no returns available. Retailers ordered only the number of comics they could sell, but soon had a steady clientele, so they could take orders and make reasonable predictions as to what they needed. This system has led not only to the revitalization of major companies, but also to the rise of several smaller, independent comics companies as well, because a comic could be profitable with a small print run, if the publisher is reasonably sure that they will all be sold.

It is among these smaller independents, or alternative titles, that we find a variety of unusual holiday and seasonal comics (some recommended for adults only) such as *Samurai Santa,* for instance, or *Weird Romance,* bearing the caption "Alien Valentine." Others are irreverent: *George and Barbara's (Bush) Christmas Crisis,* published in Kennebunkport, Maine, the former president's summer residence. Some try to nostalgically recreate the old days of seasonal comics, such as Eclipse Comic's *Springtime Tales,* which reprinted some early Walt Kelly (the creator of Pogo Possum) material. Mainstream titles have also changed, as we have seen. A 1989 issue of *Superman* featured a story called "Homeless for the Holidays" in which an employee of the *Daily Planet* is discovered to be homeless; while in 1990, *Adventures of Superman* (a different comic) carried a story in which it

While holiday comics are common, St. Patrick's Day special issues are rare. 1986.

was revealed that as a teenager, Clark (Superman) Kent was involved in a drunken driving accident after a New Year's Eve party. Kent was only a passenger, but the driver was mortally injured. The point is that there are a variety of different types of comics, and that holidays are manifested in these comics in a variety of ways. In 1986, a bizarre humor title called *Ambush Bug* had a *Stocking Stuffer,* featuring for the

first time to my knowledge the word *Channuka* on the cover of a holiday comic by one of the major publishers, in this case DC Comics.
The Legion of Super Heroes had a Hanukkah story in the 1970s,
which may be the earliest inclusion of the Jewish festival of lights in a
holiday special. Today, Hanukkah stories are commonly included in
comics issued for the December holidays.

Many comics continue their Christmas specials and summer specials; some of the alternative comic books seem to enjoy Halloween
as a holiday to exploit for its gruesome symbolism. Often, comics display a self-consciousness in their use of holidays, so that the words
"Summer Fun" are often used ironically. Some titles use the holidays
as narrative devices in regular issues, such as the New Year's Superman story described above, or DC's *El Diablo,* a Hispanic hero, in a
story set at *el Dia de los Muertos,* the Mexican and Mexican American
Day of the Dead. *El Diablo* also demonstrates another way in which
holidays can be used in serial entertainment: they can establish the
passage of "real time." That is, two issues after the *Dia de los Muertos*
issue, Christmas forms a backdrop to the story; two months after
that, Valentine's Day figures into it.

Writer Steve Englehart once wrote a year's worth of stories using
this approach. The title was *The Vision and the Scarlet Witch,* and it was
a twelve-issue limited series. (Another relatively recent development
in comics is that series are now often planned to run for a certain
specific number of issues.) In this series, each issue contains a chapter
of one continuous story, centered on a holiday or a rite of passage.
The story went from All Hallows' Day to Thanksgiving to Yule
(Christmas was clearly being celebrated in the story, but the Scarlet
Witch, because she *is* a witch, instructed another character about
pre-Christian, midwinter festivals such as the Northern European
Yule). January's story centered on Martin Luther King Jr.'s Birthday,
followed by one set in New Orleans during Mardi Gras. "Spring Fever" was next, followed by "Tax Time." The series culminated with
the Scarlet Witch giving birth to twins. Although it was not specified
in the story, the author told me that it had been his intention for the
story to culminate on Mother's Day. As I interviewed Englehart about

his use of holidays and seasons in this series, I mentioned that I thought that he was rather creative. "Tax Time," for instance, in April, was an unusual choice. He agreed, but said that as he thought about which holidays to use, he realized that April 15 (called by many IRS Day) is "a contemporary day of note" and thus appropriate (personal communication).

I agree. This leads to another point: along with the seasons (*Picnic Time, Beach Party, Winter Carnival, Springtime Tales,* etc.), official and unofficial holidays (Halloween, for instance, is not a legal holiday, but people certainly observe it anyway), other kinds of events and celebrations are relevant to this discussion. Life-cycle events like birth, marriage, and death are frequently reflected in comics. So are other occasional celebrations: a cover of *Walt Disney's Comics and Stories,* for instance, depicted Donald Duck in the Olympics. Moreover, comics celebrate their own anniversaries and landmarks: first issue, hundredth issue, fifty years of publication, and so on. Comics reflect a celebratory grid that is specific to their own industry.

Different comics have always been targeted to different age groups, and as we have seen with the famous line of EC comics, even in the 1950s some were highly irreverent and provocative in the ways they

Left: This 1994 *Sabrina's Holiday Spectacular* features a season's worth of holiday imagery: jack-o'-lanterns, a turkey, corn shocks, a bag full of toys, and a New Year's banner. In a way reminiscent of *The Nightmare Before Christmas,* the symbols are not only juxtaposed, they are mixed. A toy skeleton doll wears a Santa hat, for instance. Right: *Naughty Bits,* an adult, alternative comic depicts Santa shooting the Old Year while being attacked by the Baby Jesus. 1991.

mocked and inverted
otherwise sacred holi-
day symbolism. Many
people feel EC Comics
were the spiritual fore-
runners of the under-
ground comics of the
1960s and the alterna-
tive comic presses of
today. So comics as a
medium do not reflect a
single age group or
taste group, although it
is true that most read-
ers are males in their
teens. Nor do they re-
flect holidays in any
single way. In fact they
never did. Still, one can

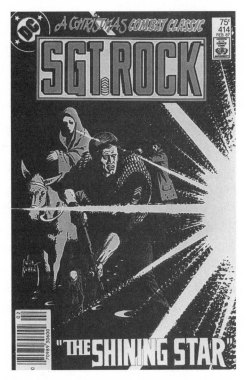

Sgt Rock's "Christmas
Combat Classic." The
range of genres of
comics is matched by
the different types of
symbols chosen for
the cover—this one
reverent and religious.
1987.

see in the comics of the 1940s and 1950s a reflection of the
schoolchild's year, while this has become less discernible in the 1980s
and 1990s. Further, if one were to create a cognitive map of the year as
perceived by comic book publishers and as suggested in their actual
publications, the holidays, life-cycle rituals, and special occasions
would vary according to the genre of comic, and would not be identical to the year as manifested in commercially available candy products. M&M Holidays, by its very name implying a direct relationship
with the annual calendar, initially gave us Valentine's Day, Easter, and
Christmas, later adding Autumn and Summer; Disney Comics quar-
terly specials gave us *Spring Fever, Summer Fun, Autumn Adventures,* and
Holiday Parade. Other comics and other candy products reveal greater
discrepancies.

Recorded music, popular and otherwise, provides us with another
area of comparison. What do we think of when we think of popular

music and holidays? "White Christmas," by Bing Crosby; Guy
Lombardo's Orchestra playing "Auld Lang Syne" on New Year's Eve;
or "Easter Parade," again by Crosby. What about "The Monster
Mash," by Bobby "Boris" Pickett? Or Chuck Berry's "Run Rudolph
Run," or the remake of it by Bruce Springsteen? Is John Philip Sousa's
"Stars and Stripes Forever," commonly associated with the Fourth of
July, to be considered "popular music"? A jazz fan might think of Louis
Armstrong's "Mr. Santa's Boogie," while the New Age aficionado
thinks of the Windham Hill releases *December,* the ongoing *Winter
Solstice* albums, or *Winter into Spring.* One might recall the *Very Special
Christmas* collections, with contributions from Bon Jovi and the
Pointer Sisters, among others, with profits going to the Special Olympics. Rhino Records has issued several collections of 1950s Christmas
rock and roll, under the name *Cool Yule.* There are rap Christmas collections, punk Christmas collections, and country Christmas collections. On Valentine's Day, love songs are appropriate, whether they
are about that holiday (like "My Funny Valentine") or not, although
artists as diverse as Paul McCartney and the Black Crowes have written Valentine's Day songs. Rhino also has two Halloween collections,
one pressed on orange vinyl in the shape of a pumpkin, the other on
black vinyl shaped like a bat. Rhino has also released a Christmas
compilation on a record shaped like a Christmas tree.

Clearly, we are again dealing with a wide variety of materials. Holidays and popular music interact in several ways. Some songs become
traditional to a specific day, like "White Christmas," to the point of
becoming a traditional part of the celebration itself, despite the commercial nature of the recording. Others may be relevant to a particular holiday because of their theme, such as love songs in February. In
this regard, for instance, RCA Records released a collection of previously released love songs recorded by Elvis Presley in February of
1988. The record was pressed on red vinyl, and the dominant color
of the album jacket was red. The release was clearly intended to tie
into the love theme of the February holiday of Valentine's Day, although that holiday itself was never actually referred to in the music
or on the album jacket. "The Monster Mash," mentioned above, is not

about Halloween nor ever mentions it, but it is about monsters and was a popular hit in the fall of 1962. It resurfaces annually in October and has become associated with Halloween. It is included, for instance, on the Rhino Halloween collection. Some songs are *about* holidays, or use them symbolically in the lyrics. "My Funny Valentine," for instance, is *not* played ritualistically on the radio every February, despite its overt reference to the February holiday.

Moreover, the songs I have mentioned obviously reflect different age groups and taste groups. All genres are represented: rap, punk, jazz, blues, country, and so forth. Bing Crosby, Chuck Berry, Elvis Presley, the Beach Boys, Bruce Springsteen, Run-DMC, the New Kids on the Block, Boyz II Men, Mariah Carey, and Kenny G all sell Christmas albums. If we extend the concept to include seasonality generally, we find significant seasonal events referred to in such disparate songs as "When the Swallows Come Back to Capistrano," or the Beatles' "Here Comes the Sun." Summer songs have always been popular in rock radio, such as "It's Summertime" by the Jamies or the Lovin' Spoonful's "Summer in the City." Many of these, in turn, reflect the rites of passage of their audiences: "School Is Out," followed by "School Is In" by Gary U.S. Bonds, or "Sealed with A Kiss" ("Now we gotta say goodbye for the summer") by Brian Hyland. Alice Cooper updated these sentiments when he sang that school was out not only for the summer but forever.

The life cycle too is represented in popular song, especially birthdays ("Happy Happy Birthday Baby" by the Tune Weavers, "16 Candles" by the Crests, "Happy Birthday Sweet 16" by Neil Sedaka, or "Birthday," by the Beatles). "Graduation Day" by the Lettermen among others shows up frequently; weddings (the Dixie Cups' "Chapel of Love," for instance) are more often pined for than realized; e. g., the Beach Boys' "Wouldn't It Be Nice (If We Were Married)" or Little Anthony and the Imperials' "I Wish That We Were Married." And of course there is death: "Our Last Kiss," "Tell Laura I Love Her," and "Patches." This latter is actually about suicide, which leads to the more recent development of an entire genre, or at least subgenre, of popular music called "death-rock," or "death-metal."

This is heavy metal music at its gloomiest and darkest, liberally using images and symbols of death. There is a band named Helloween, and another was named Samhain (after the ancient Celtic festival of the dead that is a predecessor of our Halloween). Even the names of the bands, then, are sometimes related to certain holidays, often because of the associations the holiday in question has with other imagery, such as the Satanic for Heavy Metal or the romantic for Valentine's Day. Holidays that are inversive, like Halloween, lend themselves to musical styles that are also rebellious and subversive of mainstream values such as rock generally, and heavy metal and punk, specifically.

The particular styles of music commercially available are communicated to the public in part through the graphics used in the packaging. This continues to be true, even in the era of compact discs, with their

smaller areas for design. One can get a good idea of the audience an album is intended for by the album jacket graphics alone. Heavy metal, rap, and punk all have their own distinctive graphic styles; for that matter, so do New Age, liturgical, classical, and many others. What does the year look like in seasonal album jacket graphics?

Heavy metal bands frequently avail themselves of the imagery of Halloween, such as this band, whose name is Helloween. Mid-1980s.

Easter is found chiefly in liturgical releases: *Gregorian Chants for Easter,* or *The Sequence of Holy Week,* by Johann Sebastian Bach; or in children's releases featuring Peter Cottontail or the Easter Bunny along with popular children's characters. Mardi Gras and Carnival are found in recordings of Brazilian music, in field recordings, and in the popular rhythm and blues of legendary New Orleans pianist Professor Longhair, or the Wild Tchoupitoulos (a Mardi Gras Black Indian krewe). The Wild Tchoupitoulos, in fact, are made up primarily of the

Neville Brothers, a longtime and important New Orleans musical family. In a somewhat similar way, in that the music is restricted more or less to ethnic, international, and regional releases, St. Patrick's Day shows up on recordings of Irish traditional music ("St. Patrick's Day in the Morning") and on Irish American recordings. Summertime is used as a theme in many musical efforts; here we can point to the Beach Boys' *Endless Summer* album. This band, the Beach Boys, took the imagery of Southern California and made it their trademark while frequently singing praises to the joys of the season ("We've been havin' fun all summer long"). Summer songs, popular during the all-important period between school terms for students of all ages, is a subject treated at some length in a separate chapter. Albums specifically about Halloween include the Rhino Records releases mentioned above, where the records themselves have been turned into icons of the holiday, and where the music is thematically related to Halloween, consisting of popular releases that qualify as "scary music," such as "Out of Limits," based on the theme music of the 1960s television show *Outer Limits*.

Many New Age albums are seasonally based, such as *Oktober County*. This more general approach is also found in George Winston's *December* album on the Windham Hill label. This album begins with a piece entitled "Thanksgiving," which seems to me to be a recognition of that holiday's function as the opening of the Christmas season in contemporary America. Other Windham Hill releases include several volumes of *Winter Solstice*. The musicians are never

There are Christmas albums for all types of music, including Gregorian chant and jug band music. 1987.

shown on these albums; New Age music depicts natural scenes on
the jackets. *December*'s jacket is a snowscape; while *Winter Solstice*
pictures sun rays through bare trees. *Oktober County* has a photograph
of a field of pumpkins.

Some of the most famous pieces of so-called serious music, or
"classical," or "art" music relate to the calendar in many of the same
ways we have been discussing. Tchaikovsky's *The Nutcracker* is as
much a part of Christmas as "White Christmas." Stravinsky's *Rite of
Spring* is one of the most revolutionary and important compositions
of the twentieth century, while Vivaldi's *Four Seasons* is a perennial
favorite. Some gardener friends of mine hold a "seed party" every
year, in February or March. The party is basically a kind of early celebration of the spring and its fertility. They examine catalogs and decide which fruits and vegetables they want to grow during the coming
spring and summer, often dining on food that is prepared from the
previous year's preserves, and enjoying appropriate music, including
Stravinsky and Vivaldi. In this popular usage, then, even elite music is
made a functional component of a festive seasonal ritual, and these
rituals are often personal or familial, or celebrated among a close
group of friends.

Christmas has the greatest number of musical manifestations, from
Christmas carols to recordings of Dickens's *A Christmas Carol.* There
is no genre of music that does not have at least one (but usually several) Christmas releases. Everything from Gregorian Chant to rap is
represented, so the album-jacket graphics can be easily compared.
Most mainstream, middle-of-the-road pop music albums simply feature a portrait of the artist adjacent to some seasonal symbol, for example, Perry Como framed by a wreath. This pattern generally holds
for country music, although the emphasis here is often on rural, outdoor images. Christmas is celebrated "down on the farm": musicians
ride in sleighs through snowy woods. The images reflect country
music's generally conservative, rural roots. The Christmases that
are celebrated are for the most part "old-fashioned." By contrast,
rock and roll Christmas albums often feature somewhat iconoclastic
images. Rhino Records (itself an iconoclastic label) depicts a hip

Santa doing Chuck Berry's famous "duck walk" and wearing "shades," playing an electric guitar. In a somewhat similar way, but released years earlier, *A Christmas Gift to You* (also known as *Phil Spector's Christmas Album*) considered by many the first concept album in rock (Marsh and Propes 1993, 55) featured the well-known producer of records by the Ronettes, the Crystals, and Bob B. Soxx and the Blue Jeans wearing Santa Claus garb, peering bemusedly at us over lowered sunglasses. A recently released jazz compilation depicts Louis Armstrong, horn in hand, in a Santa cap. The artist as Santa is a widely used image.

A more recent rock album is *A Very Special Christmas,* profits from which are donated to the Special Olympics. This album is unusual in that it has what must be considered a religious image: in a very stylized drawing by Keith Haring, a figure (of indeterminate gender) holds a baby. References, even broad ones, to Jesus in the iconography of popular culture at Christmastime are rare, due to the fact that not everyone in America is Christian, including many people who celebrate Christmas. In this case, though, since the proceeds from the album are intended for children, one can see the thematic and symbolic associations being made. The album jacket reminds the audience of the emphasis on charity and also of the special place of children during the season; the seriousness of purpose behind the recording is associated with sacred rather than secular images of the holiday.

Some genres recognize the issues of religious pluralism by avoiding specific reference to Christmas altogether. The Windham Hill releases discussed above are examples; they focus on natural turning points like the winter solstice (thought by many scholars to be the source event of all midwinter festivals) or simply the month of December. The parallel in comics would be the more generally seasonal Winter Fun titles, for instance, as opposed to the specifically Christmas titles. Similarly, Revels, Inc., out of Cambridge, Massachusetts, presents annual theatrical celebrations of Christmas and the winter solstice in late December that draw on both Christian and non-Christian sources and traditions. They have released several albums of materials from these presentations that draw on winter celebrations historically, interculturally, and internationally. Interestingly, they have tended toward using renditions of hearty, medieval celebrations for their graphics.

Albums featuring acoustic renditions of traditional folk music, along with newer compositions intended for acoustic performance, frequently depict a comfortable, homey scene, similar in some ways to the country albums. However, where the country albums often depict people enjoying the outdoors, these acoustic albums often show a warm, cozy room as seen from the outside through a window. On the jacket of *Pastime with Good Company,* for instance, a musician walks across a snowy landscape toward a house. We can see into the living room, where friends have congregated to play music together. The interior scene is rendered in color, while the outside is done in black and white. Likewise, the jacket of *A New England Christmas* shows a window in its center. The jacket itself, in beige, is the wall of the house. The interior is illuminated with a scene very similar to the one just described. These albums, and this style of music, uses the image of the wood frame house to suggest tradition, continuity, and perhaps old-fashioned values, and emphasizes community as the way those things are realized. Moreover, it is a community of peers, fellow musicians creating good times together in the present, *creating* community through music, rather than the implied return to one's roots that one finds in country music.

Other recordings of interpretations of traditional folk song use the circle as a design motif, signaling the sense of cyclical time, such as volume 9 of *The Folksongs of Britain.* This is called *Songs of Christmas* (Caedmon TC 1224) although it contains songs related to other times and events of the year as well. The year as circle is well represented on the jacket, as it is on another release entitled *Maypoles to Mistletoe* (Trailer LER 2092). This album features a kind of wreath whose changing vegetation represents the growth and death cycle of the year. A third album, this one by the Watersons, called *Frost and Fire: A Calendar of Ritual and Magical Songs* (Topic Records Ltd. 12T136), while it does not depict a circle on the jacket, it nevertheless takes the "all around the year" approach to the songs.

Of all the various ways companies have used traditional symbolism
to relate record albums to holidays, however, I was personally im-
pressed by the following: once I was visiting a local record store in
Bowling Green, Ohio, where I live. I began looking through the section of tapes labeled Christmas music. You never know what you will
find—in the past I have found klezmer music for Hanukkah in the
Christmas section, for instance. The clerk asked me what my interest
was, and was I searching for anything in particular? When I told her
about my interests in holidays, she asked if I would be interested in an
album that was intended primarily for disc jockey use, a sampler album featuring many different musicians, many of them wishing the
listening audience a merry Christmas. I was, so I purchased *Winter
Warnerland,* issued by Warner Communications. I did not think too
much of the picture on the jacket, a rather odd conglomeration of a
candle, two holly leaves, and what appears to be a photograph of a
reindeer's face looking like clouds in the sky. But when I opened the
album and looked inside, I found two discs: one clear red plastic; the
other, green.

While the choice of examples here is admittedly limited, they are
meant to indicate broad overall tendencies. Different genres of music
approach single holidays, such as Christmas, in different ways; the album jacket graphics show this. Moreover, different genres of music
will reflect or focus on certain holidays to the exclusion of others:
love music for Valentine's Day is found in mainstream pop, while
heavy metal rock finds much of interest in Halloween. Finally, a look
at popular music and popular periodicals such as comics, as well as
commercial products such as candy and beer, indicates that each of
these broad areas highlights different holidays and reflects a different
calendar. Even within our mass cultural forms, there is no single,
monolithic, imposed annual cycle of celebrations. The year as manifested in recorded and popular music is not the same year manifested
in comics, or in candy. Additionally, each of these reflect many different subgroups. Popular culture, then, and the mass media as well (the
two are not necessarily the same), are not quite the monolithic level-
ers of cultural diversity they are often thought to be. Just as there are

regional, ethnic, and religious diversity in the folk cultures of the United States, so is there some degree of diversity according to these factors in popular culture as well. There is also diversity represented according to age group and taste group both *within* genres of popular culture (e.g., different types of comics appeal to different audiences) and *across* these genres (if you do not read comics, you may enjoy listening to music).

Going to movies, reading cherished books, watching certain television programs and listening to favorite music of a season are ways we celebrate the holidays. Although they are not the entirety of the holiday experience, these popular forms, often of the mass media, are components of the holiday celebrations. In this way the holidays interrelate with—in fact, are made up of—movies, television, popular music, and other aspects of the popular life of America.

Chapter 3

Holidays in Media, Genre, and Popular Life

In this chapter I will discuss further some of the media and genres we looked at in the previous chapter, including comics, popular music, and film, as well as areas like politics and sports, with an eye toward presenting an overview of the many ways holidays and the seasons are part of almost every aspect of everyday life. In later chapters we will more closely examine several case studies in specific and detailed ways.

Comics

The January 1992 "Holiday Special" issue of *Archie's Pals and Gals* (no. 628) featured a four-part story called "Autumn Daze." Each chapter was devoted to a different special event, and the choices are interesting. Comics that feature several holidays during a seasonal period are less typical than specials devoted to a single celebration, and it is interesting to see which holidays are chosen and how they are dealt with. The story begins with a chapter on Halloween and ends with a chapter on Thanksgiving; no surprises there. Chapter 3, however, features the Sadie Hawkins Day race on November 9, at which any boy caught by a girl must be her date. Sadie Hawkins Day is similar to Leap Year Day in that it allows for the reversal of expected behaviors along gender lines, and was invented by cartoonist Al Capp for his Li'l Abner comic strip. The idea for this event has been picked up by some towns and turned into a real community event. Here we have an instance of the invention of a tradition within the mass media that becomes enacted in the real world. Here media is the source of a social festival.

Other, better-known examples of the influence of the mass media on the ways we celebrate would include the introduction of Ebenezer Scrooge, the Great Pumpkin, Frosty the Snowman, and Rudolph the Red-Nosed Reindeer into our holiday pantheons, and the addition of "White Christmas" to our canon of Christmas carols. However, with the above example of Sadie Hawkins Day, the effect was the creation of an actual event, something people actively participate in, from a popular fictional source. Begun in a comic strip, it has come full circle—referred to as a real festival in an Archie comic book.

Chapter 2 of "Autumn Daze" is interesting as well: it focuses on Election Day, referred to in the story as "another of fall's holidays." Archie suggests a school election to choose a student who will be Principal for a Day. The tale reminds me of the ancient English practice of declaring a Boy Bishop on the Feast of the Holy Innocents (Dec. 28), which commemorates the slaughter by King Herod of newborn babies in hopes of killing the child prophesied to be King of the Jews. Coming during the Christmas season, the day in the Middle Ages was one of total inversion of the sacred and the secular: a donkey was ridden into church, a child was bishop for a day, and generally speaking, the clergy was mocked by the common folk. This process of social inversion, in which the world is turned upside-down, so to speak, and those people who are usually powerless take control for a brief time, is found in many festivals. For instance, during the ancient Roman Saturnalia, which consisted of two weeks of celebration at the time of the winter solstice and was a forerunner in many ways to contemporary Christmas and New Year's celebrations, slave owners served their slaves.

Election Day, while still a major day of contemporary importance, ritualistic in nature, is less a festive celebration in the 1990s than it once was. In the middle decades of the twentieth century, for instance, bonfires were routinely lit for election day, a practice some feel is derived from the lighting of Guy Fawkes Day bonfires on November 5. Guy Fawkes Day is an English commemoration of the apprehension and execution of a man who attempted to blow up the House of Parliament in 1605. In some ways, the celebration has many characteristics of Halloween, including the bonfire. It is quite possible that Guy Fawkes Day grew in popularity in England as a Protestant alternative to a day viewed as Roman Catholic. Although both Halloween and Guy Fawkes Day are observed in England, Guy Fawkes Day is by far the larger celebration. It is a day of thanksgiving for the deliverance of the House of Parliament, but from a child's point of view, both Halloween and Guy Fawkes Night present opportunities for mischief, begging for money, and building bonfires and fireworks displays (see Beck 1982, 1983, and 1985).

Halloween is the Eve of All Saints' Day and is associated with Catholicism in the minds of many. England, officially Anglican, does not recognize the authority of the Pope in Rome. Guy Fawkes was a Papist, that is, a Roman Catholic, and he was part of a conspiracy that reflected these divisions along religious lines. Thanksgiving services are still offered annually in the Church of England for Fawkes's apprehension, and popularly, along with the bonfires, people light fireworks displays (said to recall the explosives Fawkes failed to ignite). Weeks in advance of the fifth of November, children build effigies called Guys, take them around, and ask for "a penny for the Guy" (see Cressy 1989).

In the American colonies, the War of Independence and the subsequent fleeing of Tories, or those who remained loyal to the crown during the war, meant that this essentially English tradition would no longer be welcome in the newly formed United States of America. Indeed, by the end of the eighteenth century, Guy Fawkes Day was no longer celebrated in the United States. It has been suggested, however, that people have shifted the November 5 bonfires to the night of the political elections.

Another comic that deals with a chunk of seasonal time is a 1958 issue of *Nancy and Sluggo Travel Time*. This is a summer comic, but the issue's stories are connected by the narrative device of noting the movement of time. The issue begins with a story about the end of the school year and the concomitant beginning of summer vacation, and ends with a back-to-school story, and includes a Fourth of July story. "School must be out for the summer!" says one character on page one. "Gee Nancy, why so glum? No more school for two months!!" says Sluggo. Nancy responds, "It's just that summer doesn't *really* start for me till I hear *fireworks* on the *Fourth of July!*" After several stories set at the beach and camp, the final story ends with Nancy mentioning to all her friends that summer isn't quite over yet, when Sluggo notices an announcement in the newspaper, "School Opens Tomorrow." "It's over now!" the children moan in unison.

Comics such as this, which deal with the seasonal flow of time rather than a specific holiday or even season (e.g., *Winter Carnival* or *Vacation Parade*) were rare in the 1940s and '50s, although there was a series entitled *Holiday Comics,* each issue of which focused on a single event, such as Christmas, Easter, a birthday celebration, and summer vacation. Other unusual comics in this regard include *Dennis the Menace Day by Day,* which takes us through a week in Dennis's life. Much more typical were the specials for Christmas, Halloween, and summer, and each of the above-named characters—Archie, Dennis the Menace, and Little Lulu—starred in comics devoted to at least one of these occasions.

Note the many ways in which comics have been tied into the seasons, after the obvious holidays were taken. It is amazing how many characters went to county fairs, for instance, including Bugs Bunny and Woody Woodpecker. Along with these were comics devoted to *Picnic Time, Winter Carnival,* and *Winter Sports.* There is even a *Little Lulu Storytelling Time,* which reflects a special time of a youngster's day, rather than year. The latter book was a special that dealt with a decidedly special time of day from a child's point of view. It also allowed the publisher to reprint a group of stories in which Lulu tells fanciful tales to her little friend Alvin.

In more recent years, comics have begun to reflect diversity, and newer special occasions. Hanukkah stories, for instance, are now regularly included in winter holiday specials; and Archie and Superman, and a more recently created character called Concrete, have all had Earth Day specials. Comics today also frequently use the seasonal progression as a structural narrative device. Sometimes the monthly sequence of holidays is reflected in the monthly publication of a series, as with the twelve-issue *Vision and the Scarlet Witch* series discussed earlier. This month-by-month succession of holidays has also been utilized by romance novel series, which regularly issue Valentine's Day, Mother's Day, summer, and a variety of Christmas-themed collections. In 1992, Harlequin published a year-long Calendar of Romance series. Interestingly, the *Vision and the Scarlet Witch* series was, in its own way, a romance. The story concerned the efforts of the title characters (one of whom is an android, that is, an artificial man) to have a child. The babies, twins, are born in the final issue, which corresponded to Mother's Day.

Comics also reflect life-cycle rites. The superhero titles, currently the mainstays of the industry, forever focus on death as an event. As a character, Death (portrayed as a young woman) had two four-issue limited series. The so-called death of Superman in 1993 received international attention (the result of both the visibility of the character and the success of the publicity efforts of Warner Communications, which owns the character). Following the death of the character, several issues of variously related titles related the "Funeral for a Friend," including one story called "Funeral Day."

Along with deaths, weddings are popular. Birth is less frequent, but a five-issue story line in *Archie's Pal, Jughead* comics was devoted to the activities preceding and during the birth of a new member of his family. Aimed at an adolescent audience, and featuring teenage protagonists, the Archie titles frequently showcase proms and similar rituals of that stage of life. Three 1993 titles—*Veronica, Archie,* and *Betty*—each featured a story on the "Spring Prom," each relating the same events from the title character's perspective. The covers of the three comics fit together to make a single large drawing of a prom.

Similarly, children's comics often feature birthday parties, while in some comics, the passage into adulthood is occasionally celebrated in comics such as *Hellstorm,* aimed at older readers.

Like many modern comics, *Hellstorm* is dark and gritty, more violent than a person who does not keep up with contemporary comics might expect. The title character, Hellstorm, is the son of Satan. One particularly violent (and very popular) character is Marvel Comics' Punisher. Featured in several titles, the Punisher also stars in summer and back-to-school specials. I cannot help but compare a *Punisher Summer Special* with the *Nancy and Sluggo Travel Time* comic mentioned above. Both have stories that take place on the Fourth of July, but the Punisher comic, published the year of the Gulf War, is full of negative stereotypes of Arabic people and sickening violence. One story ends with the Punisher mailing a dismembered finger of a villain—a finger it is strongly implied the Punisher bit off the man's hand—as a sign of the Punisher's sense of justice.

The artwork on the covers of comics is very important, since the covers are what attract potential customers. The graphics have, not surprisingly, changed a great deal over the years. Along with the sexy teacher on the cover of the *Justice League* back-to-school issue, a Halloween comic called *Seduction of the Innocent* (named for an anti-comic-book treatise of the 1950s) depicts a very sexy, very scantily clad witch surrounded by a mound of pumpkins. Close inspection reveals one of the pumpkins to be a human head.

Not all the newer comics are so extreme, however. Christmas especially continues to inspire tales of warmth and joy. *Within Our Reach* is a 1991 charity

The British Christmas song that inspired the large rock-for-charity events of the 1980s. 1984.

Christmas comic, published by Star*Reach Productions, with contributions and cooperation from all major comic book publishers (Marvel Comics' Spider-Man was licensed for use free of charge, for instance). Profits were donated to benefit AIDS research and environmental protection. This parallels the Very Special Christmas albums, which are collections of Christmas-oriented music from major artists, the profits going to help the disabled. In this regard, it is important to remember that the American Live-Aid concert to raise money for the famine-stricken in Ethiopia, and its theme song, "We Are the World," was directly inspired by the similar British effort "Do They Know It's Christmas." In all three cases, it is the special qualities of the holiday, and how the festival's symbols and meanings are constructed and interpreted, that form the basis of these activities. Such large-scale charitable efforts are entirely within keeping of traditional Christmas activities such as gift-giving. The artists donate their work; the profits are given to help others. In one sense, then, these efforts are themselves traditional Christmas activities, or perhaps more correctly, they are original and unique ways of realizing ideas that are traditional to Christmas.

The contemporary, postmodern trend in holiday-themed comics is seen in the 1992 Christmas issue of Green Lantern: Mosaic no. 9, dated February 1993. Green Lantern, a superhero, tells "the Christmas story" mixing elements from the Nativity, Dickens's Christmas Carol, Miracle on 34th Street, It's a Wonderful Life, Frosty the Snowman, The Grinch Who Stole Christmas, and Rudolph the Red-Nosed Reindeer. The synthesis of these common stories associated with Christmas into one meta-story is intended to indicate both a world-weariness and a disturbed mind on the part of the title character, but it also reflects the way Christmas is a melding together of disparate elements, some sacred, some secular, some traditional, some commercial, all of which are a part of this major annual event. In a way, the Green Lantern hodgepodge Christmas story is the postmodern American Christmas story; that is, it reflects the experience of Christmas as a pastiche of all these elements and others, both secular and sacred. This is it in its entirety:

Once upon a time, a child was born. But he was an unhappy
child, and hoarded money to the detriment of his loyal employee. Then he found an old silk hat, and when he put it on
his head he began to dance around. Seeing this, Santa asked him
to lead his sleigh, and the child believed that Santa was more
than a department store trick. He gave Christmas back to the
children, and they all toasted him as the richest man in town.
The end.

Holidays and Popular Music

In December 1992, there were three Christmas albums in the top
ten: *Very Special Christmas 2,* which was a compilation of new Christmas recordings by a variety of artists, with all proceeds donated to
the Special Olympics Foundation; along with Christmas releases by
Garth Brooks and Neil Diamond. Popular Christmas music is more
popular than ever. Ironically, a song Joni Mitchell wrote about Christmas depression has become something of a Christmas standard itself.
In "River" she writes, and sings,

> It's comin' on Christmas
>
> They're cutting down trees
>
> They're putting up reindeer and singing songs of joy
>
>> and peace
>
> Oh, I wish I had a river I could skate away on,

while the piano figure echoes "Jingle Bells." This song was used on the
Christmas-Hanukkah episode of *thirtysomething;* the ambiguity of the
song was paralleled in the conflict over ethnic traditions portrayed in
the story.

A singer and a songwriter, Joni Mitchell is originally from Canada.
She frequently uses in her music seasonal images of the North, like
geese migrating at winter. In songs like "The Circle Game" she uses
the turning of the seasons as a metaphor for life:

and the seasons, they go round and round

Painted ponies go up and down

We're captive on a carousel of time

We can't return we can only look behind

from where we came

And go round and round and round

in the circle game.

Her other songs, like "The Urge for Goin'" also use seasonal imagery in this way:

The warriors of winter give a cold triumphant

shout

All that stays is dying, all that lives is getting out

I'd like to call back summertime

Have her stay for just another month or so

But she had the urge for goin', and I had to let

her go.

Artists may, like Mitchell, use seasonal and holiday imagery suggestively, metaphorically, as in her fellow Canadian Leonard Cohen's "Sisters of Mercy" ("If your life is a leaf that the seasons tear off and condemn, they will bind you with love that is graceful and green as a stem"), or they may choose to use the months of the year and the special days of the months simply as an extended conceit, a formulaic structure upon which to hang a song. Neil Sedaka's "Calendar Girl" is a perfect example of the latter approach. Sedaka wrote and sang many popular hits in the late 1950s and early 1960s, and enjoyed a comeback in the 1970s. His work is polished, commercial, clever, and catchy. He associates each month with some event. Most are obvious: in February, she's his Valentine, for instance. Interestingly, he relates June to the junior prom. This is an example of the ways the life-cycle

celebrations and the calendrical festivals overlap. June is the month of
weddings, graduations, and proms.

I am not suggesting that one approach to songwriting is superior to
another; each has different intent, each presents its own challenges to
the songwriter, each has a place, and each can be enjoyed. Bob Dylan
combines the two in "She Belongs to Me." In one verse, we are instructed to bow to the woman on Sunday, salute her on her birthday,
purchase a trumpet for her on Halloween, and present her with a
drum on Christmas.

Musically, the song is a twelve-bar form associated with the Missis-
sippi Delta blues. Lyrically, the first two lines are repeated, and the
final two both rhyme with and complete the thought. Here, Dylan
uses celebrations to suggest character, and also to provide thematic
unity to the stanza. The 1965 Rolling Stones' album *December Children*
is an example of seasonal imagery used to help create an image for
the artists. The band is referred to as "December's children, children
of stone" in the liner notes. The Rolling Stones were cast in the 1960s
as the bad-boy alternative to the relatively more clean-cut Beatles.
December, the darkest month of the year, when skies are overcast
and dreary, suited the purpose. The Stones, the record suggested,
belonged to the dark month. A more recent use of seasonal imagery
to tell a story in the narrative of a song's lyrics is found in the Guns
and Roses song "November Rain." The accompanying video depicts a
wedding followed by a death and a funeral. Both life-cycle rituals are
contrasted: first, metaphorically in a positive way: like a rainstorm the
sorrow of death passes; and second, metonymically: the wedding is a
joyous, happy thing but (ominously, beware) it too passes, like the
cold November rain.

The Irish band U2's song "New Year's Day" on the *War* album
contains metaphorical suggestions of rebirth and renewal, as does Van
Morrison's "Almost Independence Day" on the album *Veedon Fleece*.
In both cases, the names of the holidays are used poetically. Morrison,
also an Irishman, does a song called "All Saints' Day" on *Hymns to the
Silence*. The examples are endless, but the point is that these various
songs and recordings relate to holidays and seasons differently. Some

are made to accompany the season or seasonal event. Some use the imagery to enhance the impact of the song, usually in a narrative way. Others use the imagery to create or define character, while still others use it to create an artist's image. Some are related to a season more in terms of the timing of the release than because of any association with that time.

These different kinds of uses can be extended to other seasonal objects, to things very different from music, like coffee mugs. Consider the difference between the mug that says "Be My Valentine" and the mug that says "Red Hot Lover," for instance. The former is specifically a Valentine's Day mug and can't really be sold or used at other times. The second, while relevant to and displayed during the weeks prior to Valentine's Day, can be sold and used at any time of year. It ties into certain symbolic properties, such as color (red), as well as, in this case, heart images and semiotic relationships: red hot (like the devil, like hell) and love. The same is true of music that relates thematically to certain holidays but does not specifically refer to them, such as love songs at Valentine's Day and scary music or songs with supernatural themes at Halloween.

Holidays and Popular Foods

The intersection of holidays with popular foods is one of the most rapidly expanding areas we will consider, which should come as no surprise when one considers the central place food has in festivals. Feast is part of fest (see, for example, Humphrey and Humphrey 1988). Food sales, like moneys generated by travel, are perhaps not what we think of when we mention holidays and popular culture. However, turkey, cranberry products, ham, lamb, kielbasa, matzos, kosher products, and of course alcoholic beverages and candy all enjoy brisk sales at certain times of the year. More generally, picnic foods, drinks, and accessories are heavily advertised during the summer months, especially beer.

Snack food manufacturers have begun to market for the holidays in a big way. Cereals, crackers, cookies, V-8 vegetable juice, and canned

M&Ms holiday icons
are available for many
holidays and special
occasions.

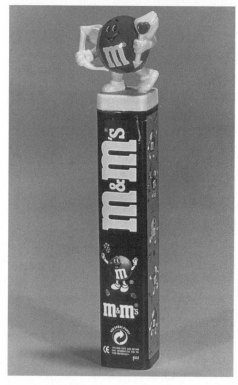

spaghetti all are marketed with seasonal packaging for Christmas, the summer holidays, and other times of year. For instance, there are Little Debbie Snack Cake products available for Halloween, Thanksgiving, Christmas, Valentine's Day, Easter, and back-to-school time. Ironically the boxes festooned with Santas and Easter bunnies are marked with the K for kosher sign. These foodstuffs indicate that the principles of serialization and periodicity found in the popular media are present in the commercial food industry as well.

As discussed earlier, M&Ms packages candy seasonally with its Holidays line. Further, M&Ms also manufactures candies in cylinders topped by toys, plastic representations of anthropomorphic M&Ms

with holiday-specific motifs, such as an M&M cupid, or an M&M holding an Easter egg or wearing a Santa suit. There was also an Olympics tie-in. When the confectionery manufacturer was an Olympic sponsor in 1992, little toy M&Ms carrying the Olympic torch, weight lifting, or engaging in a number of Olympic sports became available.

I am continually amazed at the apparently endless number of ways mass-market goods are tied into holidays and seasonality. In the summer of 1992, for instance, I saw large containers of V-8 vegetable juice and Campbell's tomato juice adorned with images of fireworks and red, white, and blue stars-and-stripes designs. Why are these drinks

Tomato juice can in the summer, featuring the fireworks of the Fourth of July. 1993.

packaged this way and released at this time of year? Presumably the corporate intent was to associate these products not simply with the summer holidays and American patriotism, but specifically with the principle festive food event of the season, the picnic. The association of these elements—Fourth of July, patriotism, and picnic foodstuffs—is widely seen at summertime, usually in newspaper advertisements for supermarkets.

The term "released" is appropriate here. Tomato and V-8 juice are available throughout the year, but cans with seasonally specific images are marketed at certain times. What we see in the case of these popular foodstuffs is an attempt to serialize items that are not periodical in nature. The Holidays candies examined above are the best examples, along with the beer promotions for Halloween, Christmas, the Super Bowl, and St. Patrick's Day. The summer-related

Christmas may be the
most commercialized
holiday of the year,
but Halloween is a
close second.

Santa Mac: Macaroni
and cheese for the
holidays! 1992.

advertising of beer is an attempt to relate beer to the season, to make the beer an associated component of the seasonal celebrations (picnics, barbecues, clambakes). It is, in effect, an attempt to make beer to summer what love is to Valentine's Day: a component capable of standing entirely on its own, but one also wholly appropriate to a certain season or type of festive event.

The serialization of commercial snack products makes them periodicals in much the same way that books and magazines are issued periodically. We expect this with popular fiction but may not have noticed its existence in the realm of popular foods. There are several ways of making sense of this. First, the seasons and the holidays are themselves recurrent, cyclical. This periodicity of the seasons and the holidays lends itself nicely to popular fiction, which always needs a new theme or subject. Magazines regularly feature stories on holiday recipes and holiday craft ideas. Many creative people find this ideal, because since the holidays are ephemeral, there is always another event to focus on, always a new reason to make something. Another tie-in between holidays and popular culture, then, is found in these home crafts and recipe publications and magazine articles. However, it is increasingly clear that a primary distinctive feature of mass consumer culture, with its ongoing need for the appearance of novelty, is the underlying principle of the serialization of virtually everything, including prepared foods.

In order to increase profits, manufacturers must forever think of new ways to sell products. In some cases the item is adapted to seasonal symbolism in a way that goes beyond the packaging, such as cranberry beer, M&Ms with holiday graphics and holiday colors, or Reese's Peanut Butter Cups shaped like Christmas trees, hearts, and eggs. In other instances, the holiday tie-in is a matter of packaging only: the cans of beer in the Jingle Bell Rock carton are the same as always. The Hershey's chocolate bar wrapped in red or green foil, the white paper outer wrapper encircled with holly, is otherwise the same as always. The festive packaging entices the consumer and rides the wave of holiday symbolism, but the product itself is no different from what it is at any other time of the year.

Little Debbie Snack Cakes are packaged for different holidays several times throughout the year. Sometimes the cakes themselves are identical. The only difference is the box: does it have a jack-o'-lantern or a pilgrim on it? This company issues ostensibly new products periodically, in a way that directly parallels popular literature. Likewise, how different from their regular product can E. L. Fudge Summer cookies be? The cookies are molded in the shapes of people engaging in summer sports like snorkeling, but otherwise the cookies are identical. This periodicization of mass-produced consumer goods may be a distinctive feature of industrial, commercial culture. The cyclical nature of the holidays lends itself to exploitation in this regard.

Politics

When President Bill Clinton delivered his Inaugural Address on January 22, 1993, he began with these words: "My fellow citizens, today we celebrate the mystery of American renewal. This ceremony is held in the depth of winter, but by the words we speak and the faces we show the world, we force the spring." Throughout the speech, the president returned to the themes of celebration, the seasons, with an emphasis on spring and the related idea of renewal. A presidential inauguration is itself a classic rite of passage, of course. It is the ritual that transforms an individual into a president. The ceremony itself is the mechanism by which this happens. It is surrounded by festival and celebration in the streets of Washington, the official and unofficial balls and parties, both in the capital and throughout the United States. With his speech, Clinton identified the inauguration as a kind of calendrical celebration that (like other winter celebrations) contains images of spring and promises of rebirth and renewal within its symbolism.

For example, Christmas has as its central religious image the sacred birth of a baby. The evergreen decorations suggest life amidst the death of winter. New Year's, like Christmas, is represented by a newborn babe, although the Baby New Year is a secular rather than sacred image. Birds and flowers are also New Year's symbols, especially those that suggest the coming spring. Both Kwanzaa and Hanukkah are festivals of light that take place during the darkest period of the year. February's Valentine's Day presents us with images of hearts (a primary symbol of life as well as love) and flowers, roses in the snow. With his address of January 1993, President Clinton suggested that presidential inaugurations can be considered as political festivals of renewal along with these other religious, ethnic, and traditional winter festivals.

Clinton said, "A new season of American renewal has begun," apparently referring to the ascent to power of the Democratic party after twelve years of Republican administrations. "Yes, you, my fellow Americans, have forced the spring. Now we must do the work the season demands." In a sublime example of the political use of the metaphors associated with seasonality, and with an apparent under-standing of the dynamic processes of renewal that frequently accom-pany ritual, festival, and celebration, the president associated the inauguration ritual with calendrical festivals. "From this joyful mountaintop of celebration," as he described it, he seems to have re-alized that the ritual was surrounded by, or framed by, play and festi-val, and, when one takes into account the millions of people watching the inaugural events on television, spectacle as well (MacAloon 1984). The very fact that Clinton's speech was based upon concepts of cel-ebration, seasonality, and renewal demonstrates both the power of these ideas and the extent to which they provide an unrecognized structure for everyday life.

Purely popular artifacts associated primarily with holidays, such as greeting cards, have political dimensions as well. Patriotic greeting cards were marketed specifically for the men and women sent to the Persian Gulf War, just as there had been similar cards for the First and Second World Wars (Holt and Holt 1987). An unanticipated re-sult of the Persian Gulf War was an increased awareness of Islamic culture, particularly the holy month of Ramadan. Due to the lunar nature of the Islamic calendar, Ramadan moves through the Western year. The lunar calendar does not correspond exactly to the time it takes the earth to revolve around the sun, so Ramadan does not fall regularly at a fixed point in the year, nor does it occur in a certain season every year. In 1990, Ramadan came in the spring, and both Easter and Passover occurred during the same period. On Good Fri-day, March 29, 1991, *USA Today* wrote about Ramadan, along with Passover and Easter, as the three major festivals of hope and renewal of the three great religions, Islam, Judaism, and Christianity. The story was featured on the front page. National popular recognition of this Islamic sacred period would never have happened, and indeed had not happened, prior to the events of the Gulf War. Since then, at least one spy novel set on Ramadan has been published, and a comic book, *The Sandman,* featured a Ramadan story. Additionally, the Gulf War brought the full commercialization of the yellow ribbon.

In the American democracy and in other countries too, politics generally are cyclical and ritualistic, especially when elections are held on a fixed day on the calendar, like the first Tuesday after the first Monday of every fourth November. Further, the recognition of only two major political parties contributes to the sports contest–like sensation of elimination that imbues our national elections. If political campaigns and voting can be regarded, at least metaphorically, as political rituals, they are also, as with the Clinton inauguration, at the center of widespread festival and celebration. Voting is an act that reaffirms the democratic system by enacting it, in a way similar to Don Handelman's concept of models of presentation: it is constitutive of the social order because the very act of voting is taken as proof of the efficacy of the political system (1990). Politics in America is its own sacred system—not religious, but still sacred—of icons (the flag), texts (the Constitution), rituals (inaugurations, state funerals), heroes, legends, and sacred history. It is no accident that campaigns and elections are conducted and victories celebrated with paraphernalia like paper hats, noisemakers, and party favors in red, white, and blue designs sold in Hallmark stores.

Perhaps the most telling use of seasonal and political symbolism that I have seen occurs on July 4 in Bowling Green, Ohio. On that holiday, many residents awake to find small American flags planted decoratively on their front lawns and gardens. These flags are placed in front of homes all over town, on the main residential streets, and every one of them carries a card that identifies—and advertises—a local realtor as the donor. In essence, this real-estate agency uses the American flag itself as an advertisement. The agency takes the connection of capitalism and commercialism with patriotism and celebration one step further than I have thus far witnessed. The realtor goes beyond embossing a product with the image of the flag or a facsimile. Rather than add the flag to the product, as has been done on cans of Pepsi-Cola and V-8 vegetable juice, for instance, the realtor attaches the name of a product—the agency—to the flag itself.

Political cartoonists are centrally important in this discussion, if for no other reason than the work of Thomas Nast, who is credited with crystallizing the appearance of Santa Claus in modern America. In a series of cartoons between 1863 and 1887 Nast presented a large, rotund, grandfatherly Santa, white-haired and great-bearded, who wore a red suit and cap, a large black belt, and boots. No longer a tiny elf, a hairy Nicholas, a Middle Eastern bishop, or a Father Christmas, Nast's Santa drew upon, but varied from, descriptions of Santa in Clement Moore's "A Visit from St. Nicholas" and Washington Irving's *Knickerbocker Tales,* and it has become the model for all later American Santas. Nast was born in the German palatinate town of Landau on September 27, 1840, and moved with his family to New York in 1846. It has been suggested that his early renditions of Santa recalled the German "Pelze-Nicol," or Hairy Nicholas figure, who, along with the Christkind, or Christ Child figure, was the Christmas gift-bearer of his youth (Paine 1904, 6). Over the years, Nast's Santa grew in stature and is recognized as the model of most Americans' concept of the appearance of Santa Claus.

Thomas Nast also gave the United States two other major national symbols, images that became permanent parts of our political rituals: the Democratic donkey and the Republican elephant. Nast first used the elephant to represent "the Republican vote" in a cartoon published in the November 7, 1874, issue of *Harper's Weekly* (Paine 299–300). As a symbol of "Democratic sentiment" (Paine, 147) Nast had used the donkey as early as January 15, 1870. In addition, he illustrated almanacs and, not unlike Norman Rockwell of a later era, was known for his annual Christmas artworks.

Perhaps Thomas Nast's most striking use of holidays is seen in a series of drawings for *Harper's Weekly* published during the Civil War. Each of these commemorated a national holiday or religious holy day, including New Year's Day, Palm Sunday, the Fourth of July, Thanksgiving, and Christmas. Each contrasted the festive event with scenes of the war in all its horror. In some cases, where real events occurred at the time of special days, the scenes depicted were of specific incidents, like Robert E. Lee's surrender at Appomattox on Palm Sunday 1865. The assassination of Abraham Lincoln on Good Friday 1865 and the "Black Easter" that followed inspired some of Nast's most beautiful work.

With regard to Nast's contributions to American culture, then, his rendition of Santa Claus has left an indelible mark, and his symbols for the two major political parties have become universally accepted. In his day, President Grant, referring to Nast's allegorical holiday drawings, commented, "He did as much as any man to preserve the union and bring the war to an end." President Lincoln referred to him as "our best recruiting sergeant" (Keller 1968: 13). In Nast, the collapsing of the popular arts with holidays, special occasions, and politics is brilliantly realized.

Illustrations by Nast and others were regularly published in periodicals such as *Harper's Weekly*. These magazines have become an endless resource for individuals such as myself, who study holidays. These line drawings of fifty to two hundred years ago show us some of the ways holidays were celebrated. They are now frequently recycled, both on commercial greeting cards and as illustrations in scholarly books.

Popular Literature

Once again, we face a vast subject and are able only to note a few interesting cases and make some suggestions. We have dealt now at some length with comic books, but before leaving that subject entirely it is worth mentioning briefly the important and closely related area of newspaper comic strips and cartoons. The daily strips mirror everyday life in ways too numerous to go into here, but some strips, such as *Gasoline Alley* or the more recent *For Better or For Worse* by Lynn Johnston take place in real time; that is, characters are born, age, marry, grow old, and die. These strips especially use the holidays as indicators of the regular passing of the years. Others, while not strictly set in real time, such as Cathy Guisewite's *Cathy*, commonly reflect humorously on calendrical occasions. For instance, a series of *Cathy* strips run during Valentine's Day week (referred to as Valentine's week in the strip) dealt with the uncertainties of relationships and romance. On one day Cathy lamented, "I bought sultry lingerie but I'm too embarrassed to wear it. I bought a suggestive card, but I'm too embarrassed to send it. . . . I bought a provocative gift, but I'm too embarrassed to give it. I thought of renting a sexy movie, but I'm too embarrassed to go pick one out and even if I did, I'd be too embarrassed to admit I had it. I'm beginning to understand why red is the color of Valentine's Day."

Other *Cathy* strips comment on seasonal time. For instance, a February 2, 1991, entry has Cathy debating with herself as to whether or not to purchase a skimpy negligée. "It's so dainty and feminine," she thinks. "Too skimpy! Too skimpy!" she counters. "So sultry and alluring!" "Too skimpy! Too skimpy!" As she walks away from the item without having bought it, the caption reads, "The February 2 shopper: a pre-Valentine brain in a post-holiday body." It is the nature of the medium of comic strips to directly reflect the flow of days, ordinary and extraordinary, of daily life.

Seasonal Skin

Even adult magazines like *Playboy* use the holidays and seasons thematically. The centerfold is sometimes holiday-related, such as a

photo layout for the July 1991 issue that featured the model posed among red, white, and blue balloons while waving sparklers for the Fourth of July. The centerfold feature was titled "Miss Liberty," and the accompanying copy read: "Wendy Kaye, the perfect patriot, is our salute to Independence Day." Year-end Christmas and New Year's issues are annual features, and

Seasonal Skin. Commercial enterprises use Santa to sell everything from soda pop to sex. 1994.

Valentine's Day imagery is frequently featured on the front covers of
February issues. These tend to emphasize the more erotic aspects of
Valentine's Day, along with the celebration of love and romance associated with it. True to its hedonistic philosophy, the magazine emphasizes the celebratory aspects of Christmas rather than any religious
content, and also emphasizes New Year's imagery in January issues
(on sale in December), because of the secular nature of New Year's
Day and the licentious aspects of New Year's celebrations. The magazine also regularly has back-to-school and spring break features.
These target the college-age group while emphasizing the bacchana-
lian aspects of the student year.

Additionally, *Playboy* publishes additional periodicals (called "flats")
every month. These are collections of thematically related photographs. Some are based specifically on the seasons: *Girls of Summer,
Bathing Beauties, Girls of Winter.* Since all the photos are of nude and
seminude models, these publications depend heavily on the accompanying captions to establish links among the photos. *Lingerie,* published
bimonthly, invariably refers to the seasons. A 1992 issue refers to
summer festivals, the Fourth, and Labor Day. One 1987 flat was entitled *Playboy's Holiday Girls,* which featured models posed in New
Year's, Valentine's Day, Independence Day, Halloween, Thanksgiving,
and Christmas settings. "Absolutely never to be accused of neglecting
holidays are *Playboy*'s Playmates, and we offer 112 pages of fabulous
photos to prove it. Whether they're popping champagne corks on
New Year's Eve or dressing in outlandish costumes for Halloween,
reading Valentines from ardent admirers or staring wide-eyed at
Fourth of July fireworks, gobbling Thanksgiving turkey or hanging
stockings for Santa, Playmates seem to possess an inordinate capacity
for having fun." Related to these are the swimsuit issues of sports
magazines, which anticipate the summer by being issued in February,
when people have had their fill of winter. Since most of us cannot afford to travel to warm, exotic locations to escape February's dreari-
ness, these swimsuit issues take us there vicariously.

Popular Novels

Certain genres of popular fiction are more likely to use certain holidays and seasons: mystery-detective; romance, suspense, and horror all regularly feature the calendrical holidays. Other genres, including westerns and fantasy, do so with much less frequency. As a genre, westerns appeal to men. Holiday celebrations are a part of the domestic religion (Myerhoff 1978) of a woman's world. As a result, we see very little evidence of holidays in western novels. In science fiction, the tendency is to invent alien civilizations complete with religious systems, including rituals. To some extent, this is also true of horror and fantasy, like Stephen King's *Children of the Corn* and Tom Tryon's *Harvest Home*. Although Tryon's book is named for a British harvest festival, both it and the King novel are in fact based on the nineteenth-century theories of Sir James George Frazer, as set forth in his famous *Golden Bough*. Although highly influential in popular life, these early anthropological speculations that invariably concern corn gods and ritual sacrifices are no longer widely accepted among scholars today.

A British novel, *The Wild Hunt of Hagsworthy,* also incorporates Frazerian ideas. It is set at a summer fete. These fetes in Great Britain usually take place in June, and are a kind of midsummer celebration. The traditional Midsummer's Day, the feast of John the Baptist on June 24, is still recognized in Britain, Ireland, and throughout much of Europe. Like Christmas, the day is thought to be related to the solstice, in this case the summer solstice of June 21 or 22. The closest equivalents to a fete in the United States are town festivals like the Weston, Ohio, Eggstravaganza or the Waterville, Ohio, Cherry Fest. There are important differences, however. The British fetes that I've experienced are church festivals and relate to the calendar in more than a commercial way; the American versions tend to be tourist-oriented and relate to the calendar only as regards tourist season. They are outdoor but sales-oriented. The competition once associated with games has transformed itself into pushing and shoving to get

on rides. Typically in the United States, people in parades now toss
candies and balloons to the children on the street. Unfortunately, one
result of this otherwise rather nice idea has been the rewarding of
aggression—those children who dominate large areas of the street
grab the most. While many older children are generous, sharing their
bounty with those younger and smaller than themselves, there is an
unfortunate tendency on the part of some to grab everything they
can. It is almost too easy to see this as American capitalism writ small,
or as an act of socialization, teaching children a kind of unspoken
American ethos about competitiveness and the rewards of aggressive
action, by means of their participation in a festive and playful ritual.
The British fetes, on the other hand, are more like the harvest
thanksgiving services in the autumn: each church has its own date, and
people from other churches attend. Likewise for the summer fetes:
churches and schools sponsor them, and people attend various fetes
in different towns and villages.

Although one can find at least one example of a book based on any
particular holiday in almost any genre of fiction, the tendency is for
certain genres to concentrate on those occasions that are most
closely related to the themes emphasized in the books. Romance nov-
elists, of course, seize upon Valentine's Day, with its love connection.
Analogously, authors of suspense thrillers avail themselves of Halloween with some regularity.

Since Christmas is the single most dominant festival in America,
despite its basis in the Christian calendar, almost all genres are represented by Christmas releases. Romances and mysteries are the most
numerous, however. I wonder if the popular literary Christmas murder mystery tradition is linked in some way to the corpus of Christmas ghost stories, of which Dickens's *A Christmas Carol* is the most
famous literary example. However, storytelling regarding the supernatural was a favorite Victorian pastime. Christmas ghost stories often emphasize rebirth and renewal along with the image of death, as
we will discuss below. The murder mysteries seem to rely more on
the juxtaposition of the grisly concept of murder with the season of
goodwill and good cheer. Nevertheless, December is the month of

the greatest darkness and is the time of the turning of the solar year, and these stories, perhaps unwittingly, pair images of death and life (murder and Christmas). So there may be a logical symbolic connection that renders this genre appropriate to this time of year.

As in other genres of mass media, popular print focuses more often on summer as a season rather than the Fourth of July as a specific celebration. Again, one finds novels of all genres related to summer, including romances, mysteries, and adolescent suspense thrillers such as *The Last Great Summer* by Carol Stanley. While this is an otherwise unexceptional novel, it is interesting in that it may typify a genre (or subgenre). *The Last Great Summer* is divided into four sections named June, July, August, and September, using the progression of the summer months as a structure on which to unfold its story of personal change and growth. (Stephen King's *Different Seasons,* by comparison, is an umbrella title invented after the fact to cover the grouping together of four unrelated short stories. In the introduction, the author relates each tale to a season, somewhat clumsily.)

The Last Great Summer has to do with graduation from high school and the transition period prior to entering college. Thus it deals with a special season framed by the school calendar and informed by life-cycle rites: graduation and, less formally, going off to college. Within that the cliché of coming of age, of growing up and accepting adult responsibilities, is carried out, but in a female domain. One character loses her virginity, another works as a nurse and faces life-and-death situations daily. Both are specifically described as becoming women (i.e., adults) as a result of these experiences. Looking at the novel as reflecting ritual, festival, and seasonal custom, we see that it works in three ways: the exploitation of the seasonal, time-out-of-time symbolism of summer; the ritual calendar of academia, including graduation from high school and matriculation in college, and personal life transitions.

It is important to note here that I am not attempting to discover any universal correlations between specific popular genres or media and various holidays or seasonal events. Indeed, upon reflection, one is struck by the apparently infinite variety of such correlations. Most holidays are manifested in most media (radio, television, film, print) and most genres (westerns, romance, mystery, situation comedy, etc.). One finds murder mysteries, for example, set on Easter, midsummer, Halloween, Guy Fawkes Night (in Great Britain), April Fools' Day, and Christmas. One line of romance novels has taken the allaround-the-year approach, and in 1992 issued a series called the Calendar of Romance, based on themes appropriate to each month. These included New Year's, Valentine's Day, St. Patrick's Day, Easter, Mother's Day, and Father's Day. July's novel was set in a New Hampshire town and dealt with both the Fourth of July and an election campaign as well. As the site of the first presidential primary of the election season, New Hampshire makes sense as the setting for a patriotic, political story. Further, it is a New England state. New England is often used as a mise-en-scène to signify associations with colonial America, 1776, the War of Independence, and patriotism. 1992 was, in fact, a presidential election year.

The novel in this way reflects the synthesis of summer and patriotism. The summer holidays—Memorial Day, Flag Day, Independence Day, and Labor Day—are all, in their own ways, civic celebrations. The flag is displayed for each of them. Commercial foodstuffs such as Campbell's Tomato Soup, V-8, and Diet Pepsi, are issued in cans with fireworks and stars-and-stripes motifs, presumably to entice consumers to purchase these items for picnics.

The Calendar of Romance titles for the rest of the year focused on the following seasonal events: in August, *Opposing Camps* was set at summer camp; September featured a "back-to-school" story about an older woman returning to school who is attracted to young "hunk" male students in a story entitled *Sand Man*. October, November, and December used, predictably, Halloween, Thanksgiving, and Christmas, but December saw several holiday releases, including two Hanukkah novels. Other publishers also included Hanukkah novels in their December holiday releases. The mass media is acknowledging the Jewish holidays somewhat more than they have in the past, when these holidays were generally ignored. A series of mystery novels by Faye Kellerman includes such titles as *Day of Atonement*, set of course on the Jewish High Holidays of Rosh Hashanah and Yom Kippur. An author named Lee Harris has written *The Yom Kippur Murder*, as well as *The Good Friday Murder, The Christening Day Murder, The St. Patrick's Day Murder,* and *The Thanksgiving Day Murder.* The author is using the holiday-ritual-celebration motif consistently, while using events that are written about less frequently than others.

Romance publishers regularly issue anthologies for Christmas, Valentine's Day, Mother's Day, and summer, the latter with titles like *Summer Madness* or *Summer Sizzlers,* or a collection of wedding stories for June, called *A June Courtship.* Along with June wedding and newlywed collections, other significant life-cycle events form the basis for collections that focus on pregnancy and childbirth as themes, for example, the romance anthology *The First Nine Months.* Each of these is related to the temporal dimension in different ways.

The Mother's Day collection says something about the readership's demographics; during the summer, people are likely to have more leisure time for reading. The summer titles also capitalize on the puns and double entendres inherent in the fact that summer is a season of much heat. A Valentine's collection makes overt the connection of romance novels to a holiday that celebrates love. *A June Courtship,* like the Valentine's Day collections, exploits cultural associations. As for Christmas, virtually every product imagin-

Mass-market fiction is also seasonally based. Mother's Day romances are joined by an unusual murder mystery collection. 1994.

able is in some way made to relate to Christmas. In the realm of popular fiction, there are annual collections of Christmas westerns, historical novels, romances, mysteries, ghost stories, and general "chillers." In 1991 there was even a publication in Great Britain called *Medical Romances for Christmas.*

Some writers of popular fiction use holidays and seasons as an ongoing motif: author Jane Haddam, for instance, has written a series of mysteries centered around particular holidays. These include *Feast of Murder* (Thanksgiving); *A Great Day for the Deadly* (St. Patrick's Day, a holiday not frequently found in popular fiction); *Murder Superior* (Mother's Day, not often used as a backdrop for murder mysteries); *Dear Old Dead* (Father's Day, likewise); *Act of Darkness* (Fourth of July); *Quoth the Raven* (Halloween); *Precious Blood* (Easter); *Not a Creature Was Stirring* (Christmas); *Bleeding Hearts* (Valentine's Day); and *Festival of Deaths* (Hanukkah). Similarly, Valerie Wolzien has written *We Wish You a Merry Murder, All Hallow's Evil,* and *The Fortieth Birthday Body,* which, while not about a calendrical holiday, focuses on a significant rite of passage; Charlotte MacLeod, under her own name or writing as Alisa Craig, has authored *The Wrong Rite* (about May Day), *Murder Goes Mumming,* and *Rest You Merry,* both about Christmas. *April Fools* and *Trick or Treat* are both by Richie Tankersley Cusick. A series written by Sister Carol Anne O'Marie, a Catholic nun, includes *Murder in Ordinary Time, A Novena for Murder,* and *Advent of Dying.* Even though these titles reflect the church calendar, *Murder in Ordinary Time* uses secular days such as Martin Luther King Jr.'s birthday and even Super Bowl Sunday as chapter titles, and incorporates the secular themes of these days into the narrative.

We also find holiday or seasonal imagery used for narrative purposes in stories not specifically intended as holiday events. For instance, Agatha Christie's *Murder in the Mews* uses Guy Fawkes Night as a plot element: it is impossible to hear a deadly gunshot amid the exploding fireworks. It is not really a Guy Fawkes Night special. The relationship between holidays and popular literature, then, parallels that between holidays and popular song. Some narratives, like some songs, are created specifically for the holidays while others involve holiday symbolism in a noncelebratory way.

Frequently, stories written (or filmed) for holidays other than Christmas borrow narrative motifs from one genre to another, one holiday to the next. For instance, a 1993 Valentine's Day romance collection contains a story about the transformation of a character who is specifically referred to as Scrooge-like, thus borrowing and recasting traditional Christmas narrative motifs for Valentine's Day. Another example is the 1995 *Batman Halloween Special,* in which Batman meets the ghosts of Halloween past, present, and future. Examples of this diffusion of themes and traditions from one holiday to another abound throughout the popular media, as with the adaptations of *It's a Wonderful Life* for a Halloween story on a 1992 episode of *Roseanne* and a 1994 Rosh Hashanah episode of *Northern Exposure,* and in the manufacturing of candy corn for Valentine's Day and Easter.

This principle of borrowing is also evident outside the mass media. A student group at Bowling Green State University once used the candy canes it had not sold in December to create a Valentine's Day item. The canes were taped to a pink sheet of paper facing each other to suggest the shape of a heart. Of course, the red and white of the peppermint sticks were appropriate to the Valentine's

Representing a diffusion of motifs from one holiday to another are these Halloween candy canes, colored orange and black. 1994.

Even toilet paper is
available for the
holidays. 1994.

Day holiday. Candy companies now produce candy sticks in colors appropriate to other holidays, often with a rubber toy attached to one end. One can buy orange candy sticks with bats, ghosts, devils, or witches on the end: a commercial adaptation of the Christmas candy cane to Halloween. The students' heart-shaped candy canes are an unofficial adaptation of Christmas candy to Valentine's Day. In the students' case, their use is productive in that it recycles leftover holiday items that would otherwise have no use. Fiske would see the Halloween peppermint sticks as supportive of the existing hegemonic order and the Valentine candy canes as resistant to it (Fiske 1989). As a folklorist, I would term the former an official usage and the latter a folk usage.

The flying of flags and banners with seasonal imagery is another example of the borrowing of customs from one holiday to another. These flags can be homemade, locally produced, or manufactured for national distribution. Seasonal flags are among the most re-

cent developments in holiday decorating, suggested perhaps by liturgical banners used seasonally in some churches. I would have thought
that the repertoire of Christmas decorations was exhausted, which
might explain in part why other holidays have grown in popular support. However, the use of seasonal flags represents yet another addition to the vast range of decorations already available to us.

In a consumer society, there is a basic need to provide the illusion
of choice and novelty, thereby keeping the economy stimulated (see,
for example, Jameson 1991). The holidays, with their deeply familiar
images, are a convenient way of achieving this continuing novelty. I
wonder, though, if there is not some deeper appeal to periodicity;
why so many aspects of the commercial culture of the United States
have become serialized, on the model of a television series or a magazine. Genre fiction, especially romance novels, is issued on a monthly
schedule in the same way that magazines are, and in the way that the
old pulp fiction magazines once were. Reading a contemporary romance or mystery paperback, one does not simply enjoy the novel as
a pleasure in and of itself. One becomes a part of a sorority or fraternity, a world centered around a genre, a publishing company, a continuing character. The intrinsic parallels between the unending turning
of the season (and the concomitant sense of familiar progression
through the year) and the serialization of the reading experience
(with the ongoing sense of looking forward to what comes next) are
realized in the Harlequin Romance Calendar of Romance series described above.

Sports

Each professional sport has its own grid for its season. These correspond more or less closely to the summer, autumn, winter, and
spring. Baseball, for instance, is thought of as a summer sport, although the initiation in February of spring training in advance of the
playing season is held by many as an early indication of the coming
change in seasons. Opening day is directly related to spring, and is
referred to in newspapers and television newscasts as a ritual opening

of spring at least as frequently as are seasonal celebrations such as Easter. Most of the season is played during the summer months, but the playoffs are in early fall, and the season culminates in what is called the October classic, the World Series. Regardless, as Roger Kahn's popular 1972 novel *The Boys of Summer* and the film made of it indicate, baseball is equated primarily with summer. Football, on the other hand, is an autumn game, although here again, the official season begins in early September and ends with the Super Bowl in late January. The football season begins in the heat and frequently culminates with games played in the snow. Hockey, played on ice, is associated with winter (and colder climates), while basketball is played throughout the spring months. One year I heard a radio announcer in Washington, D.C., pronounce basketball officially a summer sport, because the final game of the championship series was played on June 21, the first day of summer. He was implying that the season had been extended far too long.

Professional sports are big business, of course, tied intimately to television. The Super Bowl, often referred to as an unofficial national holiday, is a product of the marriage of professional football with television. It began in 1967 and is entirely a product of the television age (see, for example, Real 1977). In fact, those who insist on referring to it as an unofficial national holiday are representatives of the media, those people whose interests are best served when vast numbers of people watch the game. That is, the television broadcast industry seems to be most intent on establishing Super Bowl Sunday as some kind of folk or popular holiday, not the people. It is paradoxically a kind of official unofficial holiday, in that its impetus comes from the entertainment media and sports industries.

College sports are big business too, both in terms of revenues generated from broadcast rights on television, and also in terms of generating alumni donations to the educational institutions. Still, college and university sports are more closely tied to the seasons because the academic year itself is closely based on the seasons. Classes are conducted in fall and spring. Semester break is somewhere between mid-December to mid-January. Spring Break in March allows thousands of young people to journey to sunny climes for a week. Shorter (and thus different, special) courses are held during the summer.

One reason professional sports push the limits with regard to the appropriate time of year for playing certain sports has to do ultimately with money, but primarily with expansion. New team franchises are awarded to competing cities, and, to accommodate the increased number of teams, the playing season might be lengthened, as in football, or new divisions created, as in baseball. As we have seen, each sport has its internal calendar, with preseason games, opening day, opening day at home, playoff eliminations, and championship games. Baseball has the All-Star game as a midseason ritual. Sports are a major area of popular culture, and in addition to the relationships of sporting events to calendrical holidays (the practice of watching football games on Thanksgiving and New Year's Day, for instance), each sport has its own calendar with its own set of rituals, significant markers (such as the All-Star break), and truly spontaneous celebrations (as when a team wins a championship).

Hallmark Holidays

Many customs we practice at Christmas and midwinter today can be dated back at least as far as the time of the Roman Saturnalia. These customs include decorating homes with evergreen, giving gifts, and lighting candles. Another custom we associate today with Christmas and New Year's also had its parallels in ancient Rome: exchanging greeting cards. In the Rome of Julius Caesar, people gave each other tokens and coins expressing good wishes for the coming year. Also, emperors minted coins with their likenesses bearing holiday wishes. In fact, we inherited the contemporary January 1 New Year's date from Julius Caesar, who initiated reform of the calendar then in use. The Saturnalia, a major annual festival, was celebrated for ten days beginning at the time of the winter solstice. Caesar established the date of the new year as beginning at the end of the period of festivities.

New Year's tokens, though, and New Year's gifts as well, preceded the Roman Empire and are found in other ancient cultures of the Middle East. After the time of high Roman civilization, the forerunners of greeting cards in woodcuts, coins, and other tokens were known through the Middle Ages. For instance, a fifteenth-century German woodcut depicts the infant Jesus on a donkey, bringing glad tidings for the New Year. The first commercial Christmas card is thought to have been printed in 1846, in England. Greeting cards have become big business in today's world, and are universally associated with contemporary holiday celebrations. In fact, along with flowers and candy, greeting cards have been called the principal medium of celebration in America (Schmidt 1991). Still, as often as people criticize the card companies for their roles in commercializing holidays, it is important to realize that, like so many other contemporary holiday customs, exchanging tokens of greetings at the end of the year did not originate with Hallmark, Norcross, or American Greetings.

People send cards for Christmas, for Valentine's Day, at Easter and Halloween and Thanksgiving, and of course Mother's and Father's Days. More recently, Grandparents' Day has joined these other occasions. As a result, people have begun to view all holidays cynically, as phony concoctions foisted upon the public by the greedy greeting card, floral, and candy industries. Schmidt has traced the widespread development of Mother's Day in America to massive promotion efforts by the florist industry, despite the fact that Anna Jarvis, who essentially created the day in memory of her own mother and lobbied for its acceptance on the national calendar, denounced such commercialization. While it is true that Mother's Day was the brainchild of an individual acting on her own, the way the occasion is celebrated in the United States today is primarily the result of very purposeful and direct campaigns by the commercial flower and greeting card industries (Schmidt 1991).

Ironically, the companies that derive the greatest profit from such recently invented holidays generally suggest that these days are, essentially, folk celebrations. Sweetest Day, which has some popularity in Ohio, for instance, was supposedly invented by a Cleveland man who distributed gifts to that city's orphans on a Saturday in October. The story is vague and is perpetuated by card companies. According to Bart Holbrath, supervisor of corporate communications and public relations for American Greetings in Cleveland, Sweetest Day is "a day to celebrate the meaning of relationships, friendships, and a special person's nearness." While Sweetest Day, observed on the third Saturday of October, seems popular in Ohio, at least among college students, it also appears to be entirely supported by greeting card and florist industries (Cummings and Bridges 1985). From the industry perspective, events like Sweetest Day are not created by business concerns, but rather, businesses are responding to the growth of their popularity. According to this rhetoric, these industries are merely responding to popular demand rather than manipulating it. While I have suggested a similar perspective on the commercial aspects of Halloween, Christmas, and the others, there is a continuum extending from observances that have been recently invented by commercial interests, on the one side, to fully traditional popular celebrations on the other. Many events, clearly, are somewhere in between these two poles, but Sweetest Day is closer to the former.

Although Sweetest Day enjoys some popularity among the college set in mid-October, it is not widely celebrated or even known. Part of the reason for this, I believe, has to do with the nature of the event itself. It takes place approximately two weeks before Halloween, a holiday that is heavily candy-oriented. Further, the overt rationale for Sweetest Day—recognizing one's loved one—is replicated by the much older and better-established holiday, Valentine's Day (which is also quite popular among college students, since so many of them are of courting age). However, both Halloween and Valentine's Day are well-integrated into the seasonal calendar; both take on meanings from the time of year at which they occur. Further, Halloween and Valentine's Day seem to reflect timeless issues of culture, having to do with death and harvest (ghosts, skeletons, pumpkins) in the one case, and love and life (hearts, flowers) in the other. Sweetest Day has no such traditional symbolism nor any deeper cultural significance. Simply put, it doesn't work.

Not every industry-sponsored innovation does. Nevertheless, holidays have become so totally identified in the public's mind with the greeting card industry that the term "Hallmark holidays" has entered the popular vocabulary. While this term privileges only one greeting card manufacturer (albeit a major one) it is somewhat unfair for other reasons as well. People usually use the term to refer to the recently invented occasions I mentioned above, but a cloud of suspicion has also covered other holidays. The extent of commercialization connected to holidays in America is so vast that many people feel there may be nothing of any real value remaining in them.

Greeting cards are closely associated with Valentine's Day, Christmas, Thanksgiving, Easter, St. Patrick's Day, and, increasingly, Halloween. Cards are readily available for important Jewish festivals including Hanukkah and Passover. Cards can be had for Chinese New Year and St. Joseph's Day, and are sold in diverse foreign languages. Business in greeting cards is lucrative and expanding. During the Persian Gulf War in 1991, as in both the First and Second World Wars previously, patriotic cards were available to send to loved ones in military service. Greeting cards are being marketed that reflect new, African American celebrations and rites of passage. Greeting cards, then, represent to many people the best and the worst of contemporary holiday celebrations: at their best, they reaffirm social networks by expressing love, concern, and good wishes to friends and loved ones, while at their worst they represent commercialization, profiteering, and runaway greed (see Papson 1986).

Yet the exchange of greeting cards is not a part of all holidays. We do not send cards at the Fourth of July, for instance, even though it is one of the major national holidays. Likewise, cards are not generally mailed for either Memorial or Labor Day. Summer seems to be a time when personal and familial rites of passage like graduations, confirmations, and weddings take precedence over the national holidays. Cards are purchased in large numbers for these ritual events. Also, the summer vacation requires the mailing of postcards to friends and family. These are the summertime parallel to the Christmas card, and again, they are seasonal rather than holiday-specific.

On the other hand, even though Christmas cards are still sold in enormous volumes, cards geared to other midwinter events are growing in popularity. New Year's cards are making a comeback (they once were more popular than Christmas cards in the nineteenth century), along with the above-mentioned Hanukkah cards, and even winter solstice cards are available. These various alternatives to Christmas cards reflect the cultural pluralism of the population of the United States. They also indicate a growing awareness of that multiculturalism by the card industry. In this, the industry is responding to a very real social dilemma. Although not every American is Christian, it is very difficult to be American and not celebrate Christmas (see, for example, Miller 1993). It is both a national and a religious celebration. One result of this conflict has been the development and elaboration of other ethnic, religious, and personal celebrations in December. Hanukkah, biblically and historically a minor Jewish festival, has become elaborated in the United States in part as a response to the dominating Christmas festival. Also, the other developments can be viewed as a kind of resistance to the hegemony of the dominant culture as well. Since the late 1960s, a growing number of African Americans have celebrated Kwanzaa, which begins on December 26. Many atheists observe Solstice Day instead of Christmas, with Solstice trees, the exchange of gifts, and, as we have seen, solstice cards. Frequently, all that is involved in these instances is the renaming of the custom. The Christmas tree becomes the solstice tree, for instance. In cities and towns across America, Revels, Inc., offers as midwinter rituals pageants and performances that incorporate both Christian and non-Christian traditions. The greeting card companies reflect these trends in their products.

The changes in social roles are also seen in greeting cards, which can now be found "for the two of you together," indicating a couple living together; cards for gay couples; cards for Christians to send to

Jews at Christmas; and vice versa. These too indicate the growing
awareness of diversity in the United States, a diversity that was always
there but is becoming increasingly apparent.

The growing numbers of Halloween cards indicate another area in
which social trends are reflected, in this case the dramatic growth in
popularity of a long-standing traditional holiday, with the corresponding increase of participation in it by different population groups. The
sheer volume of Halloween cards available in October is enormous.
They come in all styles: humorous, off-color, sedate. There are Halloween cards to send to Mom, to brothers and sisters, to your children, your wife, your husband, or the person you live with. Walk into
a card store in October and you will be met with a sea of orange and
black. The growth in the number of Halloween cards purchased and
sold corresponds to a more general growth in the popularity of that
holiday since the 1970s (see Santino 1983, 1986, 1994b). Is the industry responding to a change "from the bottom up," that is, on the
popular level, or is this yet another case of the industry in fact creating that change? That is a primary question whenever commercial
industries and cultural change are discussed, and the answer varies
according to particular situations. The popularity of Halloween is due
to a variety of factors, including its intrinsic symbolism and position
on the calendar, the maturing of the baby-boom generation, the cultural pluralism referred to above, and many other things, including but
not restricted to industry efforts to commercialize it. Unlike many of
the industry-sponsored commemorative days, Halloween is not a
newly created occasion. It is centuries old, ancient in several aspects.
Its popularity has grown from the late 1960s to the present, a period
that has involved changes in lifestyles, population, and demographics
that led to the exploitation of the celebratory opportunities found in
Halloween. The aging of the baby boomers referred to above, a generation who were in certain ways unwilling to put away the things of
childhood, along with the growing need for a nationally celebrated
nondenominational holiday marked by the traditions of masquerading
and inversion, made it ideal for elaboration. Gay people have known
this for years, and the large urban costumed celebrations of today

were immediately preceded by urban Halloween processions of elaborately attired cross-dressers.

Meanwhile, some of the post–World War II customs like trick-or-treating were undergoing transformation as, increasingly, people live in apartment buildings, condominiums, and neighborhoods where one does not necessarily know one's neighbors. Distrust of strangers has led to suspicion of Halloween treats; unsubstantiated rumors of poisoned candy and apples laced with razor blades have led to a change, if not a decline, in the actual practice of trick-or-treating (Grider 1984; Best and Horiuchi 1985). However, other customs have grown in popularity, as Halloween has become celebrated more by adults. The numerous Halloween greeting cards are a measure of the remarkable popularity of the day and the many different types of people who enjoy it.

Some holidays are more suited to the custom of exchanging greeting cards than others. Valentine's Day, obviously, depends on it. The central custom of the day involves the exchange of love notes that are named for the patron saint of the day. History has it that the first documented Valentine was sent in the fifteenth century by Charles, Duke of Orleans, who was imprisoned at Agincourt, to his wife, while legend maintains that the custom began with an imprisoned St. Valentine in ancient Rome. These stories are very shadowy and often contradictory. The skeleton of the story is that Valentine was a Christian during the reign of Claudius II, an emperor who held to the traditional Roman religion. Valentine was imprisoned for actively practicing Christianity. According to some stories, he was a priest who continued to secretly marry people, even in captivity. Other stories say that he was in love himself, and sent letters to his paramour signed "from your Valentine."

We may never know the truth of any of this, but Valentine's Day is at least partly derived from old Roman and European festivals held during the late winter and early spring period. The Roman festival of the Lupercalia is probably one such influence on the modern Valentine's Day. Among other things, the Lupercalia featured images of fertility and sexuality, corresponding to the turning of the season to a time of growth. In the modern world we have translated this sexuality to frilly Victorian images of romantic love, although the more overtly sexual nature of Valentine's Day is beginning to reassert itself.

Since the primary customs of St. Valentine's Day involve declarations of love, the commercial greeting card is perfectly suited to this holiday. Candy, of course, is involved in one way or another in just about all our holidays, and Valentines' Day is no exception. In fact, the formulation of candy, cards, and flowers as the three mainstays of contemporary American holiday celebrations is as evident here as any other time of the year. Valentines *are* cards. Along with them, we may choose to give a box of chocolates and a bouquet of roses. All of these are tied into Valentine imagery; we all know the heart-shaped candy packages. The roses, or other flowers, may have something to do with the old symbolism of the coming spring that the day has inherited. Candy is sweet, an attribute that allows for any number of puns. Also, people increasingly speak of chocolate as an aphro-

Matchbooks too can be turned into holiday items. Circa 1960.

THE TIMMONS
O'DELL, MARGE,
BILLY and BONNIE

Merry Christmas

disiac, an association that is often used in contemporary Valentine cards.

Valentine's Day then is perfectly suited to exploitation by the greeting card industry. So is Christmas, a time when we affirm certain familial and social networks by exchanging gifts and sending cards. The first Christmas card dates from England in 1846. By the end of that century, Christmas cards had surpassed New Year's cards in popularity as the Victorian Christmas grew to overshadow New Year's as the major year-end, midwinter festival. Today they have become a major part of the annual round of festivities. The Postal Service in the United States, and in other countries as well, regularly issues special Christmas postage stamps. Significantly, both Christian and non-Christian images are always made available, again reflecting the deep duality of the sacred and the secular that comprises Christmas. For non-Christians, however, all images associated with Christmas reflect the Christian tradition. In this way, for many people Santa, Rudolph, and Scrooge represent the religious holiday; they are not truly secular figures. The issue of what is sacred and what is secular with regard to Christmas continues to be debated. For many people, the concept of a non-Christian or secular Christmas symbol is a contradiction in terms.

People keep special lists of names and addresses of Christmas card recipients. People sometimes speak of having only a "Christmas card relationship" with someone they haven't seen in years. Indeed, Christmas cards do reflect social networks, but in a rather interesting way. Who *don't* we send cards to? Our colleagues at work? While recognizing that generalizations are impossible to make, one's Christmas card network seems to reflect old friendships and older relationships. People employ other means, like parties, to ritually mark relationships with people we interact with daily and socialize with frequently. Christmas cards are for neighbors, and faraway or very close family and friends. People often send cards to people they haven't seen in years. In fact, every so often we may consider weeding some names out of the annual mailing list. There comes a time to stop sending someone a card, on the basis that no real relationship exists anymore.

There is always the embarrassing experience of deciding not to send someone a card, only to receive one from that person shortly before Christmas, leaving us scurrying about to hurriedly mail a card in time for the holiday.

There are many reasons one sends Christmas cards. Sometimes it is done out of social pressure, other times out of a sense of necessity. A person might not like one's supervisor at work, but feels it expedient to acknowledge the boss regardless of personal feelings. People do not always like or respect the recipients of their greeting cards. Nevertheless, many of the relationships in an individual's life are reflected in the people who are sent cards: family, distant relationships, professional relationships, friends. Perhaps family relationships make up the majority of card recipients: uncles, aunts, cousins, nephews, and nieces. Christmas is a holiday that emphasizes family (note the central religious image of the Holy Child, surrounded by mother, father, and in decreasing importance, shepherds). Sending Christmas cards reaffirms these ties. Often the card is the only affirmation of this bond all year; marking those relationships by sending cards becomes very important.

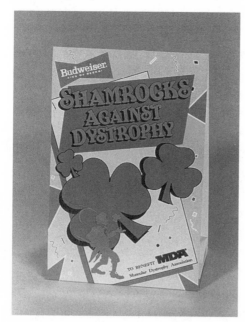

Beer companies frequently capitalize on the tradition of drinking on St. Patrick's Day in their advertising. In this case Budweiser has gone a step further by using the shamrocks as symbols for a good cause. 1993.

Other holidays that emphasize family, including Thanksgiving and Easter, also do a lot of business in greeting cards. Halloween is interesting with regard to greeting cards. Unlike Christmas, Thanksgiving, Passover, Hanukkah, or Easter, the day does not celebrate the nuclear family, at least not quite in the same way. Unlike those other festivals, there is no prescribed meal as part of the celebration. Despite the roles of parents in Halloween, children, adolescents, and adults tend to celebrate it among peers, whether by trick-or-treating, attending parties, pranking, or parading in costume through the streets. The popularity of the holiday itself, its development as one of the major celebratory days of the contemporary calendar, a kind of national Mardi Gras, has encouraged the greeting card custom (which is associated with holidays generally) to become one of its components.

Halloween cards are useful for illustrating another way in which greeting cards reflect relationships. The style of any particular card chosen reveals something of the relationship. A person chooses a different card for her grandfather than for her lover. Cards can be risqué, romantic, nostalgic, funny, gross, or overly sweet. They present certain images and symbols associated with a holiday, and these in turn are keyed certain ways. That is, do you choose a drawing of a bunny rabbit or a rendition of Christ crucified to send as an Easter card? How those images are presented is equally important. A humorous card parodying a sacred image may be less appropriate for one's mother, for instance. The choice of card we send reveals something of the way we ourselves view both the recipient and the nature of the relationship.

The price of the card, too, might be taken into consideration here. When I was growing up, our family regularly received a Christmas card that was noticeably more expensive than most. It called attention to itself with its gold-embossed paper. The sender's name was professionally printed rather than personally signed. The card was viewed with some admiration for the distant relative who had done well for herself, but the respect was limited by the ostentatious nature of the card. Its gaudiness appeared to us excessive and unnecessary, as if the sender was trying too hard to make a statement about her economic status with the card.

Although there has been an upsurge of popularity of Halloween cards in the 1980s and 1990s, such cards have been popular in the United States since the first decades of the twentieth century. Graphic styles have changed, but Halloween postcards from approximately 1910 to 1920 depict essentially the same images we associate with Halloween today. However, they sometimes refer to customs that are less well known. One card, for instance, shows a girl in the long, conical hat that has become associated with witches. Beside her are two black cats, also in witches' hats. Two owls are shown. Beside her is a basket of apples, while the clock behind approaches midnight. In her hand she holds—what? It is hard to make it out. When I ask people what they think it is, their first response is that it is a snake. In her other hand she is holding an apple. A closer look reveals that the mysterious object is an apple peel. The girl is tossing the apple peel over her shoulder at midnight on Halloween, in the belief that the peel will spell the initials of the future spouse. This is an old belief, more a game, really, that is still practiced in Ireland and parts of the United States, although it is not widely known here. In this way, the card documents not only traditional symbols, but also games, beliefs, and customs associated with Halloween. For those who are not familiar with the customs in question, it is difficult to interpret the card.

Many older greeting cards are like this. Some feature images that seem wrong for the holiday in question. Others show images whose referents are forgotten. One mysterious Christmas postcard from about 1910 depicts two birds hungrily eyeing a crawling beetle. The verse gives no hint as to the appropriateness of this scene to Christmas. Other old Christmas cards typically depict summer scenes, for instance, sometimes with an accompanying verse like "May your year be sunny and bright," which reveals the connection: in its function as a year-end festival, a good Christmas augurs well for the entire new year.

Some Christmas cards printed in the first two decades of the twentieth century could easily be mistakenly thought to refer to other holidays today. One looks like a contemporary valentine, another looks like it's a Thanksgiving card. Styles change, and symbols that appear obvious to us today may be meaningless to our grandchildren's generation. Who is to say, decades from now, that people will auto-

matically recognize or understand why we sent cards with a picture
of a reindeer with a big red nose?

Most of our holidays have certain traditional symbols associated
with them, such as hearts, evergreen, candles, and jack-o'-lanterns.
These images are often quite old. They have become associated with
certain days on the calendar through a combination of historical
events and symbolic meanings. Old as they are, these symbols are
continually reconceived in novel ways on greeting cards. Very often
what changes over time is the graphic or artistic style in which the
card is rendered, rather than the actual symbols used. For instance,
some recent valentines reveal a variety of styles and contemporary
images. One features a personal computer, for instance. Another depicts a tanned, apparently well-to-do couple playing tennis. Some are
overtly suggestive. All of them, however, use red as a dominant color
and depict hearts. The computer shows the traditional heart pierced
by an arrow; the tennis game implies a pun with the term love, while
the female player wears a heart dangling from a chain. On another
card, an attractive woman suggestively holds—fondles—a giant pencil,
while standing in the middle of a heart. Other recent valentines up-
date the image of Cupid. Some show scenes of masqueraders, recalling the holiday's origins in European carnivals. The cards are all very
contemporary in artistic style, and reveal changes in social attitudes
toward sex and toward Valentine's Day itself, but they all use the very
old and traditional symbolic language of Valentine's Day to do it.

Some holidays have a historical depth that is quite ancient. The
symbols of Halloween, Christmas/New Year's, Valentine's Day, and
others have been associated with these occasions for centuries, even
millennia, and are deeply meaningful within the context of the celebrations. Thus, a good deal of valentine imagery is traceable to the
ancient Roman Lupercalia and has to do with the fertility of the awakening earth. Halloween draws powerful images of harvest and death
from centuries of celebration, going back to ancient festivals of the
dead such as the Celtic Samhain and of the harvest among other
sources. The candles, gifts, and evergreens of Christmas and New

Year's were found among the Romans before the coming of Christianity. These and other such symbols have deep resonance for people still: the lighting of candles in late December, for instance, corresponds to the time of the winter solstice and the darkest days of the year. The decorative use of evergreens is done at a time when most vegetation is dead. These symbols offer the hope of sustained life while the world sleeps a deathlike sleep, and they offer light at a time of darkness.

Chapter 4

Summersong

When does summer begin? According to our calendar, which origi-
nated with Julius Caesar and was revamped under Pope
Gregory the Great, June 21 is the first day of summer in
the Northern Hemisphere. This is also the usual date of
the summer solstice, a solar phenomenon that occurs
when the sun crosses an imaginary line into the tropic of
cancer, or, saying it another way, when the sun reaches
its southernmost point relative to the earth in its orbit.
The result is the longest day of the year; that is, the day of
most daylight. After the summer solstice, the amount of
daylight in any twenty-four-hour period grows shorter by
day, imperceptibly at first, noticeably after a while. The
point at which the amount of daylight and nighttime are
equal occurs when the sun "crosses" the equator. This
happens twice each year, on or about March 21 and September 21. These are the spring and autumn equinoxes.
These dates mark the beginnings of spring and fall according to the Gregorian calendar; while December 21, the
winter solstice, the day of the least amount of daylight,
marks the beginning of winter.

However, very few of us actually experience the seasons this way. In many parts of the United States, summer
weather precedes June 21 by weeks. In fact, Memorial
Day weekend is said to be the unofficial beginning of sum-

mer, with Labor Day its close. In terms of mass commercial culture, the first wave of motion pictures that studios hope will do big business during the summer months is released on Memorial Day weekend. The ritualistic nature of these holiday weekends as rites of passage into and out of a season—summer—that exists in sharp distinction to the others is underscored by such customs as dress codes. It is said to be fashionably incorrect to wear white shoes at any other time of the year, for instance. So we have special articles of clothing that signal a special time, and this time exists not from June 21 to September 21, but from Memorial Day to Labor Day.

Summer—the entire season—is a time out of time, and not just for students and teachers. Even though people work their regular schedules, summer is when we vacation, when we establish and reestablish ties with friends we consort with only during the summer. Summer is when we take walks in full daylight, after supper is done. Summer is when we go away for weekends as often as possible, when children go to camp, when teenagers have summer romances, when we all have midsummer's night dreams.

Although the Gregorian calendar is gradually being adopted for use by countries all over the world, other calendars for measuring time are still in operation, such as the Jewish and the Chinese, for instance. These coexist with the Gregorian. Others have been replaced by it. Such is the case with the ancient Celtic peoples, whose descendants today include the Irish, the Scottish, and the Welsh. Prior to converting to Christianity in the early centuries after the life of Christ, the seasons of the Celtic calendar were summer, from May 1 to August 1; harvest or autumn, August 1 to November 1; winter, November 1 to February 1; and sowing, or spring, February 1 to May 1. In Britain, and especially in Ireland, today we can see traces of the old calendar and evidence of the overlay of the Gregorian. If summer is reckoned from May 1 to August 1, then the solstice is the midpoint of the season. It is midsummer. Likewise, the winter solstice occurs in midwinter, not at the beginning of the season, as in the Gregorian calendar. Most scholars believe that the celebration of Christmas on December 25 is ultimately related to ancient celebrations of the winter solstice. Likewise, June 24 is the feast of St. John the Baptist, who prepared the way for the coming of the messiah. St. John's Eve, June 23, is Midsummer's Night, the fabled night of magic as chronicled in Shakespeare. Once again, scholars feel that the celebration of Midsummer's Night is derived from the celebration of the solstice.

So again we ask: when does summer begin? Probably at a different time for each of us. For schoolchildren—and their parents—summer most likely is felt to start when school is out for the year. I remember the chanted schoolyard countdown: "Ten more days and we'll be free, honey, honey, ten more days and we'll be free, babe." And of course, "No more pencils, no more books, no more teachers' dirty looks!" once the last day of school actually arrived. As a college professor, I still live in the academic year, and for me summer begins when spring semester's final grades are turned in.

I think it is no accident that Neil Sedaka aligns June with the junior prom in his song "Calendar Girl." Late spring and early summer is a time filled with rituals of the life cycle: proms, graduations, first communions, and confirmations. Further, June is the month most in demand for weddings, and as such has become conventionally associated with lovers in songs of the June-moon-spoon variety.

Magazine covers feature seasonal symbolism. This June 1913 *Ladies Home Journal* uses the rite of passage of graduation as a seasonal event.

Moreover, graduations, or commencements, as they are also called, have taken on a kind of national ritualistic character, similar to the way Memorial Day has. That is, graduation ceremonies are regularly reported in the national media, on television news, in newspapers, and in magazines. The speeches of the commencement speakers are excerpted for us all to savor. It matters not whether we ourselves are graduating, or are related to anyone graduating, or even know anyone graduating, for that matter. These commencement rituals are presented as meaningful to us all. The events themselves are of course transitional for the participants, who move from being students to being adult members of society through the agency of the ceremonies. When broadcast nationally, I think the transitional nature of the ceremonies is being extended to refer metaphorically to the transitional time of the year: it is the beginning, or commencement, of summer. It is another way of marking the end of the old year lived indoors and the beginning of a special time of outdoor life, including backyard barbecues and beach parties. A visit to the card shop at this time of year reinforces this thought. The racks are filled with cards for weddings, confirmations, christenings, bar mitzvahs, and graduations. The life cycle seems to correspond to the seasonal cycle at this time of year.

Summer has been celebrated in song for centuries, from "Sumer Is Cumin' In," which dates to fifteenth-century England to "Summertime," a 1991 rap song by DJ Jazzy Jeff and the Fresh Prince. In fact, summer is second only to Christmas in terms of numbers of popular songs devoted to it (see Milberg 1993), which supports the idea that while the winter season is dominated by the Christmas holiday, summer as a season dominates the Fourth of July. One example of this, for instance, is found in Coca-Cola advertisements. In December, Santa Claus is depicted drinking Coke, but in the summer, the sun itself holds the famous soft drink. Songs—and other forms of mass media—about Christmas are many; songs about winter are fewer and often subsumed under the category of Christmas songs, such as "Winter Wonderland" and "Frosty the Snowman." Inversely, songs about summer are legion; songs about the Fourth of July are rare.

In the folk songs of England and Ireland, the "merry month of May" is usually presented as a summer month, with summer imagery. In many of the old British ballads, the central actions occur in May. The month is often used to create contrast with the events described, as in the well-known "Barbara Allen":

> 'Twas in the merry month of May,
>
> When greenbuds all were swellin'
>
> Sweet William on his deathbed lay
>
> For love of Barbara Allen.

In other songs the season is connected to images that were understood to refer to lovemaking, sexuality, and fertility, as in "Spotted Cow":

> One morning in the month of May
>
> As from my love I strayed
>
> Just at the dawning of the day
>
> I met with a charming maid
>
> "Good morning to you, wither?" said I,
>
> "Good morning to you now."
>
> The maid replied, "kind sir," she cried,
>
> "I've lost my spotted cow."
>
> "No longer weep, no longer mourn,
>
> Your cow's not lost, my dear,
>
> I saw her down in yonder grove
>
> Come love and I'll show you where."

Other traditional songs exploit the symbolism of June and the work traditional to it, intimating, as in "Spotted Cow," a sexuality appropriate to the season. For instance, "A Rosebud in June" juxtaposes the roses coming into bloom with the chores of plowing and sheepshearing:

> It's a rosebud in June,
>
> and a violet in full bloom
>
> and the small birds are singing

Love's songs on each spray

We'll laugh and we'll sing, love

We'll dance in a ring, love

As each lad takes his lass

all on the green grass

and it's all to plough where the fat oxen graze love

as the lads and the lasses do sheep shearing go.

"Ploughing" with one's lass in the field, along with the images of flowers and June, are metaphors weighted with symbolism of sex and fertility. Perhaps the "June-moon" songs are not as recent as we thought. Similarly, the British folk song "John Barleycorn" consciously ties the planting, growth, and harvest of that cereal to the death and rebirth of a fertility figure in a tongue-in-cheek homage to the making of "home-brewed ale."

They've laid him in three furrows deep,

They've put upon his head

And these three men made a solemn vow

John Barleycorn was dead

They let him lie for a very long time

'Til the rain from heaven did fall

Then little Sir John he sprang up his head

and did amaze them all

And they let him stand 'til the Midsummer Day

'Til he looked both pale and wan

Then little Sir John he grew long beard

and he so became a man

The growth, harvest, and preparation of the barley crop is described in anthropomorphic terms, and the song ends with the results:

They worked their will on John Barleycorn

But he lived to tell the tale

They pour him out of an old brown jug

and they call him home brewed ale.

In the United States, summer officially begins not on May 1 but at
the time of the summer solstice, usually June 21. The image of the
solstice is used in various genres of popular music in a number of instances, including jazz, New Age, and folk. In each of these instances,
the solstice seems to represent nature itself, rather than culture (as a
reference to a specific holiday might) with implications of unmediated
natural experience flowing from direct personal encounter with solar
and celestial events. Both New Age and jazz compositions parallel the
improvisational nature of the performances with the natural but significant solar event; while Tim Hart and Maddy Prior's *Summer Solstice*
album, a collection of contemporary interpretations of traditional
British folk songs, uses the solstice to create an image of an earlier
day, a merry day uncluttered by the poisons of postindustrial life—
poisons both environmental and political. In short, the image is one of
a golden age when the songs recorded on the album were presumably
sung as part of everyday life.

The summer solstice shows up in popular rock and roll as well: Jan
and Dean recorded a song of that title, and Seals and Crofts hinted at
it in their recording "Hummingbird" when they refer to the days
growing longer and the sun's rays growing stronger. They describe
this as a new day dawning. There is a nice thought here, that the turning point of the longest day can be for all of us a source of personal
renewal. This idea is repeated in other songs as well, including another Seals and Crofts song entitled "Summer Breeze."

First, however, a survey of some of the popular songs of summer
will indicate some of the other themes and ideas commonly associated with summer, and will allow us to see how summer itself is con-
strued in various kinds of popular music. In turn, this should indicate
some of the ideas about summer we hold as a society. For instance,

the spiritual renewal held in the rays of the sun, as hinted at by Jimmy Seals and Dash Crofts above, finds its analog in the suntan industry. The billions spent in advertising tanning products and in buying such products, as well as the time spent lying in the sun in search of a tan (despite frequent warnings from health care professionals concerning the dangers of skin cancer involved in such activity) is sometimes referred to as a kind of contemporary sun worship. I think it is more correct to see it as the result of ideas and beliefs, usually unarticulated, concerning the regenerative power of the sun, as well as ideas we hold regarding ideal standards of beauty and the perfectibility of the human body. Tanning is thought to transform us, or at least those of us who are Caucasian, and a discussion of summer and popular culture would be incomplete without a mention of this industry and the customs and beliefs associated with it. *Playboy* centerfolds modeling for suntan lotion advertisements are as much a part of the popular culture of summer as are the books we read, the movies we see, and the songs we listen to during that time.

As we have seen, songs that celebrate summer have been a staple of popular music for centuries. In more recent times, rock and roll has had summer songs since the middle 1950s, when the Jamies sang "It's Summertime." Many of the summer songs reflect the student's calendar, as mentioned above: Connie Francis's "V-A-C-A-T-I-O-N" is framed by Gary U.S. Bonds's "School Is Out" and "School Is In." "Summertime Blues," Eddie Cochran's classic rock and roll song, covered by many other musicians, including The Who, is a catalog of teenage complaints connected with being young:

> I'm a-gonna raise a fuss, I'm a-gonna raise a holler,
> About a-workin' all summer just to try to earn a
>   dollar.
> Ev'rytime I call my Baby, try to get a date,
> My Boss says "No dice, Son, you gotta work late."
> Sometimes I wonder what I'm a-gonna do
> But there ain't no cure for the Summertime Blues.

Often these songs recognize a special quality of the summer as a season like no other, a "time out of time" (Falassi 1987). Regular relationships are suspended; as the Tempos sang in 1960, "See You in September." On the other hand, summer romances bloom: "Now we gotta say goodbye for the summer, but darlin' I promise you this: I'll see you every day in a letter, sealed with a kiss. . . Now it's gonna be a long, lonely summer." In one of her earliest efforts at recording, songwriter Carole King worked this theme in a song called "It Might As Well Rain Until September" (because her boyfriend has gone until then). In 1980, the Rolling Stones took what is for them a typically male-chauvinistic view of these temporary liaisons in their "Summer Romance": the woman has to go back to school, while the song's protagonist will still be sitting by the swimming pool. The summer romance is over, Mick Jagger sings in a sneering, gloating tone of voice.

Sometimes the summer brings separation because we go to camp, as Allan Sherman's early sixties' "Hello Mudda" reminds us:

> Hello Mudda, hello fadda
>
> Here I am at Camp Grenada
>
> Camp is very entertaining
>
> and they say we'll have some fun when it stops
>
>   raining.
>
> Take me home,
>
> Oh mudda fadda
>
> Take me home,
>
> I hate Grenada. . . .

Sometimes it rains, as in "Summer Rain" as sung by Johnny Rivers in 1970. In that song the persona speaking in the lyrics recalls dancing all summer to "Sgt. Pepper's Lonely Hearts Club Band." The song reminds us that summers can be defined by popular songs. The Beatles' famous album *Sgt. Pepper* was not about summer, but was a summer album in a different way: It was released in June for summer business, in much the same way as the movies mentioned above. Like the summer film releases, it is tied to the season according to an annual eco-nomic cycle. Also, it is tied to summer temporally, in that, because it was released when it was, it became popular during the summer. *Sgt. Pepper* was successful beyond anyone's expectations, but like many other popular recordings, it has become linked in people's minds with a particular time. This particular album attracted so much attention worldwide that it became synonymous with the summer of 1967, the famous summer of love, peace, drugs, and hippies.

This is a common phenomenon, identifying certain summers with the songs that were popular on the radio. How many of us remember our adolescence this way? Should a survey such as this one include summer hits such as, say, 1965's "Satisfaction," by the Rolling Stones? Should it include songs about certain specific summers, like Scott McKenzie's "San Francisco (Be Sure to Wear Some Flowers in Your Hair)," or the Animals' "Warm San Franciscan Nights," or Pink Floyd's "Summer of '68"? All of these are worth mentioning as we explore the myriad ways popular culture, in this case popular music, interrelates with holidays and seasonality through the year.

Many songs simply celebrate summer, such as "Summertime" from *Porgy and Bess* by George Gershwin, Ira Gershwin, and DuBose Heyward; Nat "King" Cole's "Roll Out those Lazy, Hazy, Crazy Days of Summer (Those Days of Soda, and Pretzels, and Beer)"; or the 1991 rap recording "Summertime" by DJ Jazzy Jeff and the Fresh Prince. Chicago's "Saturday in the Park," while it refers to any pleas-ant day, compares the exhilaration of a sunny day in the park to the Fourth of July. Like the Cole song, "Saturday in the Park" celebrates the festivity of summer itself, and it is in this regard that the chief holi-day of summer is mentioned, while a southern summer in which "fish are jumpin' and the cotton is high" is sketched in Gershwin, Gersh-win, and Heyward's "Summertime." In classical music, Musikfest has released a compilation entitled *Fireworks Festival,* which includes Handel's famous *Music for the Royal Fireworks.* In 1993 Angel Records released *A Summer Concert in the Park,* with selections from George Gershwin, Jerome Kern, and John Philip Sousa (including the perennial favorite "Stars and Stripes Forever"). A novel feature of this album is that it includes recipes from *Victoria* magazine "to help you create a memorable picnic for your own summer concert in the park." The recipes are for tomato Provençal sandwiches, cucumber sandwiches with mint butter, and strawberry tea. In rap, DJ Jazzy Jeff and the Fresh Prince carry on the popular summer song tradition nicely; they offer their own gentle description of summer madness, one that includes family reunions, playing basketball in the park, looking for women, and women looking back. Summertime is itself an aphrodisiac, they conclude. DJ Jazzy Jeff and the Fresh Prince's summer rap contains many of the themes noted in other summer songs, including the ideas of being out of school, summer as a time for love, seasonal rituals like family reunions, and the idea of summer as uniquely distinct from the rest of the year.

Summer—the entire season—has a special quality to it. Certainly the above songs attest to that. The Lovin' Spoonful, a band popular in the 1960s, also deals with this subject, but in a somewhat different way. Their hit "Summer in the City" describes the Manhattan heat beating down on the back of one's neck. Anyone who has ever spent a summer in New York city can relate to this, and in what has emerged as a consistently exploited theme in summer songs, the lead singer John Sebastian sings that summer is a special time, a different world, and the time is right to find a woman to love.

The Lovin' Spoonful were not the first to sing of the city heat. Where do you go in New York to escape it? According to the Drifters, "Under the Boardwalk" down by the ocean. Since summer is dominated by the sun, songs like the above-mentioned "Summer Rain" contrast summer with either rain or other seasons for dramatic effect. Chad and Jeremy's 1964 song, "A Summer Song" contrasts the falling leaves and rains of autumn with memories of summer, as does the Roy Orbison song "Our Summer Song." These songs contain references to the summer romance that, during the summer days and nights, seems as endless as summer itself, but which, like summer, passes. With summer's end we return home, where Brian Hyland and

Carole King wait patiently for our return. The images of rain and autumn suggest this passing, this return to everyday life.

Conspicuously absent from this essay so far have been the Beach
Boys. If a band can define the summer in the way that the Beatles did
with *Sgt. Pepper's Lonely Hearts Club Band,* so can the summer define a
band. More precisely, a band can use the symbolism of the beach and
the sun and the surf and the endless summer in defining and presenting itself. The Beach Boys did this. Led by Brian Wilson's songwriting,
this musical group associated itself with, and became the chroniclers
of, the Southern California surfing scene, to the point where they
found it difficult, if not impossible, to shed their image as they experi-
mented with other styles of music. They are a paradoxical band: despite their "teeny-bopper" image, they were the first American band
to produce their own recordings. Not only is Brian Wilson's
songwriting highly regarded by critics, but he also made important
contributions with his studio production as well. In fact, it was the
Beach Boys' album *Pet Sounds* that Paul McCartney wanted to top
when the Beatles began work on *Sgt. Pepper.* Moreover, Brian Wilson
is a troubled individual, apparently schizophrenic, and ironically, despite all the songs he wrote and the Beach Boys recorded about
surfing, Wilson himself was afraid of water and never surfed. Still,
through their sound and their image, their words and music, the
Beach Boys have become the embodiment of the endless summer
even as they age. They portrayed summer as a time of freedom, of
thrills, of "miniature golf and Hondas in the hills . . . We've been having fun all summer long," they sing. In 1992 the Beach Boys redid Sly
and the Family Stone's funk hit "Hot Fun in the Summertime" on an
album called *Glorious Summer,* but summer, as seemingly endless and
paradoxical as the Beach Boys themselves, ends.

School is in. We are having a Labor Day picnic to welcome new
students to our M.A. program. Football season's begun, but I'm more
interested in who is going to make it to the World Series. It looks
as though the Red Sox are going to break my heart again this year,
but at least that means I'll have free time to watch some of the new

shows on TV. Fall also brings with it new film releases, music releases, and rock tours. It's back-to-school time. Halloween candy and costumes. Thanksgiving turkeys and travel. The weather at the cookout is summer-hot, but it is the department's annual fall picnic. Despite the continued onslaught of heat and sun, summer is over.

Chapter 5

Autumn Death and Winter Rebirth

Throughout this book we have referred to the ways holidays are reflected and used in popular narratives of all sorts. Shakespeare's *Midsummer Night's Dream* and *Twelfth Night* would be two relatively early examples of this, for let us not forget that Shakespeare wrote his plays to be seen and enjoyed by the greatest number of people. He was first and foremost a popular artist as we have been using the term. In fact, it is thought that early drama arose from religious ritual, and certainly medieval church dramas such as the mystery plays, which deal with the birth of Christ and are performed at Christmastide, have a strong relationship to church liturgy. The same is true of earlier Roman and Greek dramas, which were performed in front of temples of worship. The relationship of these dramas to the religious calendar necessarily focused them on seasonal celebrations, since religious calendars are themselves sacred interpretations of the year. As we will see in this chapter, the folk art of mumming is another kind of ritualistic popular drama intimately associated with the seasons.

The various approaches to holidays we saw in music and comics are found in films too. Movies such as *Holiday Inn* (1942), *Meet Me in St. Louis* (1944), and *Sweet Heart's Dance* (1988) all use the passage of the year as a narrative structure, employing the special days as a means of mov-

ing the story along (note the confused turkey in the animated November scene in *Holiday Inn,* because President Truman had changed the date of Thanksgiving to allow for an earlier start of Christmas shopping). *Fried Green Tomatoes* (1992) tells us what time of year it is, and suggests time's passage, by changing the decorations at a nursing home in every scene in which an elderly woman is visited by a younger character. I noted this when watching the movie with friends (on New Year's Day). After the visits at Halloween, Christmas, and Valentine's Day, the next such scene showed no obvious holiday iconography, other than more general spring flowers and pastel colors. However, it turned out to be the woman's birthday.

Chi-Chi's restaurant features a drink of the month. Since it is a Mexican restaurant, Cinco de Mayo is one. These pictures also show the tendency toward exploiting the sequentiality of the calendrical holidays. 1994.

These are examples of what I have termed the "all around the year" approach, wherein the fictional work moves through the full annual holiday cycle. Some films display this sense of movement, of the passage of time, within a few months rather than the entire year. *Sleepless in Seattle* (1993) is one such movie. The main characters are initially introduced in Christmas Eve scenes, as the female lead takes her fiancé to meet her family in Baltimore. They announce their engagement during dinner. Afterwards, they drive separately to Washington, D.C., for Christmas Day with his family. Along the way, the character played by actress Meg Ryan hears a tearjerking personal story on a national radio show about a recently widowed man and his son.

The action shifts to New Year's Eve. The actions of the male and female leads, Tom Hanks and Meg Ryan, are paralleled; both are seen sitting on a dock, yearning for something missing in their lives, making wishes as it were, while New Year's festivities go on around them. There is in the turning of the year from old to new a sense of openness, of possibility, of magic, and also of destiny. Folk beliefs abound describing how actions performed at the magical midnight moment can determine the events or fortunes of the upcoming year. The practice of making New Year's resolutions is related to this idea. The thought seems to be that at midnight, the moment that belongs to neither the old year nor the new, yet is both at once, we can wish ourselves to be something we are not. We can make ourselves over. *Sleepless in Seattle* exploits the symbolism of New Year's in this regard: at the magical turning point of midnight on New Year's Eve, wishes can come true. Possibilities are open, endless. The characters are clearly destined to meet; their destiny is shared.

The primary holiday that drives the story, however, is Valentine's Day. A subplot that runs throughout the film is that the story parallels that of a Cary Grant movie entitled *An Affair to Remember* (1957). In that earlier film, actor Grant tells female lead Deborah Kerr to meet him at the top of the Empire State Building on Valentine's Day. In *Sleepless in Seattle,* Tom Hanks's son arranges for the two adults to meet at the top of the Empire State Building on Valentine's Day, which happens at the culmination of the movie. Our final vision is of the Empire State Building dominating the Manhattan skyline as the camera pulls back, certain windows illuminated with red so as to form a giant heart. Although it was released in the summer, the probability is that *Sleepless in Seattle* will forever be enumerated among lists of love stories for Valentine's Day.

Interestingly, the summer of 1993 saw the release of another movie set on the holiday of a different season: *Hocus Pocus,* a comedy about three witches on Halloween. Again, although released out of season, *Hocus Pocus* will very likely in the future be listed in popular guides and newspapers as a good film for fall viewing. In one sense, then, both *Sleepless in Seattle* and *Hocus Pocus* are summer films, in terms of their release dates. In terms of their narrative content, however, neither of them belongs there. Likewise, 1994's *The Crow* was a summer release, but the narrative takes place on Devil's Night, a Detroit Halloween tradition. The Devil's Night celebration, and Halloween generally, with its fundamental imagery of the return of the dead, provides an important ambiance to the plot and the primary character, who has returned from an unquiet death to avenge the murder of his lover. Detroit's Devil's Night involves widespread acts of arson. It is an aggressive, violent, destructive take on Halloween, combining the traditional imagery of the fires of Hell with the danger of hobgoblins and tricksters. The content of *The Crow* is correspondingly violent and aggressive. The choice of Devil's Night as the time of the story is very intentional, and adds suggestive dimensions to the action.

Films frequently use specific holidays for purposes of plot and character exposition, as in, for instance, Woody Allen's *Hannah and Her Sisters* (1986). In that film, Thanksgiving dinner is used as a kind of leitmotif, recurring three times over three years in the movie. On each occasion, characters have changed status: newly married, divorced, realigned. The Thanksgiving dinner gathering is used as a kind of snapshot that captures the kaleidoscopic rearrangement of the family members from year to year. The nature of Thanksgiving dinner with its emphasis on family relationships foregrounds these ever-changing roles. Allen also uses Thanksgiving dinner to good dramatic purposes in *Broadway Danny Rose* (1984), and he has contributed *A*

Midsummer Night's Sex Comedy (1982), based in part on Ingmar
Bergman's *Smiles of a Summer's Night* (1955), to the canon of movies
that celebrate that season.

So many movies use holiday scenes creatively, as part of the narrative flow. *Lady and the Tramp* (1955) begins and ends on Christmas;
Lady, the cocker spaniel, is a Christmas gift. Similarly, *101 Dalmations*
(1961), another animated Disney dog film, concludes with a Christmas scene. *The Addams Family* (1991) begins with the misanthropic
title characters pouring boiling water on carolers (this borrowed
from the original Charles Addams cartoons), and has a Halloween
scene as well.

Other films are of course *about* Christmas, or Halloween, or other
specific holidays, such as *Miss Firecracker* (1989), which is set on the
Fourth of July, or *Planes, Trains, and Automobiles* (1987), which is an
exaggerated, comic account of traveling home for Thanksgiving. Many
films are felt to be appropriate to a particular holiday without being
directly about it. *1776* (1972), for example, is broadcast on television
around the country at Independence Day; *The Luck of the Irish* (1948)
with Tyrone Power, around March 17. Biblical epics such as *The Robe*
(1953) and *Ben-Hur* (1959) are felt to be appropriate at Easter. The
point to be made here is that while there are no universal rules regarding the correspondence of these culturally specific events and
materials, neither are these relationships entirely arbitrary.

For instance, John Carpenter chose Halloween as a temporal setting in which to frame a film about a murderer who is apparently supernatural, returned from the dead; Halloween is the day when the
souls of the dead are traditionally said to roam. The film, called simply
Halloween (1978), was very successful, and spawned numerous imitations. These, using Carpenter's *Halloween* as a model, were set on
other special days and ritual occasions of the year, such as *New Year's
Evil* (1981) and *April Fool's Day* (1986). While none of these other holidays or rituals are as specifically identified with images of evil in the
way that Halloween is, all contain the quality of the suspension of ordinary events, of "time out of time." Thus, in Carpenter's *Halloween,*
the so-called slasher genre was identified in an organic way with an

annual festival that features symbols easily appropriated by the genre;
then, in a secondary way, that film became a model for others that
continued to exploit certain characteristics of ritual and festival for
the purposes of the films. Sometimes the process involves inverting a
holiday's symbols rather than reinforcing them; that is, along with
calendrical occasions similar to Halloween, filmmakers have used
more ostensibly cheerful occasions like Junior Prom night or Christmas for such films. However, in these cases, familiar and reassuring
events and figures such as Santa Claus become frightening. The tension is created by inverting the symbol, taking the comforting event
and making it threatening.

Of course, Santa Claus has not always been the jolly old elf of
modern American mythology. In ages past, he was a punisher as well
as a gift-bringer, frightening as well as comforting. Some critics have
seen in the slasher Santas a kind of psychological balancing out, a recognition of the "dark side" of Santa Claus. I am not so sure of this; if
this era and our culture defines Santa as a kindly, avuncular figure,
then that is what he is for this culture. Symbols are created by people.
Though they have histories, their meanings are constructed in contemporary social contexts. On the other hand, Santa can easily be
seen as a kind of parental deity or substitute. And as we all know, as
much as we love them, parents can be very frightening at times.

Horror Films and Holidays

With the success of John Carpenter's *Halloween,* a great number of
horror films have been set on holidays, during life-cycle celebrations
or occasions of marginality. Not only have there been several sequels
to the original *Halloween,* but we have also been treated to
Pumpkinhead (1988), *Friday the 13th* (1980, set at summer camp), *April
Fool's Day* (1986), *Graduation Day* (1981), *Hell Night* (1981), *Silent Night,
Deadly Night* (1984, Christmas), *Camp Sleepaway* (summer camp,
which has also been used as a scene for comedies, such as *Camp
Candy*), *New Year's Evil* (1981), and so on. These films are commonly
referred to as slasher films, although Dika has argued that they com-

prise a specific genre she terms "stalker films" (1990). In her otherwise well-done treatment of these films, however, she only briefly
mentions the fact that the action of these films invariably occurs on a
holiday or during a rite of passage of some sort. The reason for this,
she suggests, is due to the comfort and stability of these occasions:
that is, the eruption of the horrible into the mundane events of everyday life is rendered that much more terrifying if these events are ones
that we feel fond of and nostalgic about. I suggest that, while this may
well be true, there is a great deal more going on as well.

First it must be said that the success of Carpenter's *Halloween,*
which came as a surprise to the film industry, set the model for the
later films. In other words, one way of imitating Carpenter's film was
to use a holiday, celebration, or ritual of some sort as the setting.
Since Halloween was already taken, others had to do. However, it is
significant that one of the first such special calendrical occasions utilized was April Fool's Day, a day that, like Halloween, is customarily
marked by pranking and tricking; that is, by the inversion of social
conventions.

Halloween is an obvious choice for an occasion upon which to set
a horror film. The day itself celebrates images of death, evil, the supernatural, the macabre, and the diabolical. On Halloween the spirits
of the dead are said to be wandering; what better night for a deranged, almost supernatural, killer to be stalking his prey? The belief
in Halloween as a night of the wandering dead is quite ancient. Traditionally it is a time for turning social rules upside-down: children take
the streets and demand treats of adults; adolescents soap windows
and throw eggs while police look the other way; gay people publicly
parade their sexuality; and images of death and evil, which we might
otherwise be uncomfortable with, adorn middle-class suburban
homes and are worn as costumes. These activities, and the history of
the day, indicate that Halloween is a time not merely of inversion,
when social rules are turned upside-down, but of liminality, when social rules are suspended entirely.

A good deal of the liminality of Halloween has to do with its ancient status as a new year's day; that is, that it occurred at the turning

of the year. Even today, it retains its status as a seasonal, if not annual, transition point in many areas of the country. Such turning points are often anomalous, neither here nor there; "betwixt and between," in the famous formulation of anthropologist Victor Turner (1967, 93–111). As we have seen in the discussion above, midnight is a good example: it belongs to neither one day or the next, yet it belongs to both at once. Such marginal, anomalous points are often perceived as dangerous and uncontrollable; thus midnight is termed the witching hour. Moreover, such transitional points often attract ritual, religion, and supernatural belief as a response to their marginality. Halloween was once such a turning point, and to some extent still is. A result of its transitional nature is manifested in beliefs that the barriers between the world of the living and the world of the dead were opened, and that the souls of the dead roamed this world.

The celebrations of our lives also mark turning points: birth, puberty, graduation, marriage, retirement, death. Each of these turning points has accompanying ritual to ease the transition. And virtually all calendrical holidays, life-cycle rituals, and celebrations of special occasions have the quality of liminality. They all, therefore, are open-ended: the barriers are down.; regular social categories are suspended for the period of the event. This is true of graduation, when one is no longer a student but not yet an adult; it's true of a stay at summer camp when one is away from home and family, in a strange, natural (not cultural) setting, with a group of peers who may not know each other. That is why ghost stories are particularly frightening when they are told around a campfire: the fear of the unknown in the content of the story reflects the context of the telling. As for prom night, not only is there a film named for it, but Stephen King made good use of it in the novel and film version of *Carrie* (1976). It is during the prom that Carrie's telekinesis powers erupt, after she has been drenched in blood as a practical joke. Additionally, the blood has been associated with menstruation and the concomitant social and psychological maturation process. Thus King exploits that particular rite of passage in the story as well.

Friday the thirteenth, of course, is a day widely associated with bad

luck. Both the day and the number have traditional, negative associations, for reasons lost in time. Friday is the weekly holy day for Mus-
lims; it is quite possible that it gained negative notoriety among Jews
and Christians for this reason. A more recent interpretation, in the
Christian context, holds Friday to be an unlucky day because it is the
day when Christ was crucified. Likewise, there are a number of suggestions as to why thirteen is considered an unlucky number. Some
point out that it is a number that can be divided only by itself and the
number one. Although there seem to be ancient numerological associations of thirteen as a number having some power, there is also,
again, an explanation based on Christian belief. According to this,
Christ and his twelve apostles together number thirteen, but one of
those apostles, Judas, was a betrayer of Jesus. Thus, the addition of
the one traitor to the twelve good people made thirteen an unlucky
number. The ultimate explanations probably have to do with all of
these factors and associations, and others as well. Whatever the case,
the occasional intersection of the number thirteen with the day Friday
is considered particularly ominous. It is this quality of danger and marginality that the *Friday the 13th* films exploit for dramatic purposes.

Some rituals and holidays lend themselves better to this sort of
movie. *Halloween,* of course; also *April Fool's Day,* because of the social
inversion intrinsic to the customs associated with the day (it's accept-
able to fool your friends and for the media to knowingly present
false information). *Hell Night,* referring to fraternity hazing, has the
appropriate name; the title *Pumpkinhead* associates the movie with
jack-o'-lanterns and thus with Halloween. Others are less adaptable.
Although Christmas is marked with periods of license (eating, drinking, and partying in excess are tolerated), New Year's Eve carries
much more of the socially disruptive behaviors (thus the film, *New
Year's Evil*). Christmas certainly has its share of supernatural beliefs
associated with it—the miraculous is fundamental to accounts of the
holiday—but the values celebrated at Christmas are those of social
cohesion, such as peace on earth, goodwill toward all, rather than the
celebration of death and the dark, underside of life found during Halloween, or the licentiousness and intoxication associated with New

Year's Eve. As a result, the attempt to use Christmas as a setting for a slasher film in *Silent Night, Deadly Night* (1984) was met with a great deal of resistance and outrage on the part of the American public. Nevertheless, there had been other Christmas slasher films prior to *Silent Night, Deadly Night,* such as the Canadian *Black Christmas* (1975), also known as *Silent Night, Evil Night*, in which sorority sisters are murdered by a mysterious intruder who just might be Santa Claus. *To All a Goodnight* (1983) has a plot similar to *Black Christmas.* A 1980 film called *You Better Watch Out* depicts a Santa who punishes the bad with lethal force. *Don't Open 'Til Christmas,* another in this genre, was released the same year as *Silent Night, Deadly Night.* At least one writer has speculated that the twisted, evil Santas of these films are a nod toward the pagan underpinnings of Christmas itself, a reflection of some of the supernatural elements of that festival that seem to have been sanitized out of recognition by the modern sentimentalization of it.

Whatever the case, Christmas was probably chosen more for the shock value of using a usually joyous, comforting occasion and introducing an element of the horrible into it, than capitalizing on imagery intrinsic to the occasion, as in Halloween. In between these two extremes, however, lie the other films, and I would suggest that both principles are operative in each of them: the extension of the anything-can-happen quality of ritual and festive events, along with the blasphemous effect of introducing figures of terror and evil into familiar surroundings. Certainly, the principles of marginality, liminality, and transition are closely related to the thematic appearances of evil, deranged killers in these films that are regularly set at and named for life-cycle rituals and calendrical celebrations.

The Halloween festival is not always used as a setting for horrific events in films. However, when it is used in a movie, the magical qualities of Halloween are usually capitalized on in one way or another. In Steven Spielberg's *E.T.* (1982), for instance, boys first fly through the air on a bicycle on Halloween night, against the backdrop of a gigantic full moon. Likewise, although there are some slasher films that are set on Christmas, most Christmas films are quite different in nature. In this regard they reflect the differences between Halloween and Christmas. Both holidays are focused on children, but on Halloween, children take control, go outside, demand treats from adults, and may play pranks on them. At Christmas they play with their toys and sit down to a large family meal. If Halloween suggests death during the season of the harvest, Christmas suggests ongoing life through the winter (with evergreens) and rebirth, through the Christian symbol of the newborn Messiah.

The Nightmare Before Christmas (1993) juxtaposes these symbols dramatically. The film is a curious anomaly: it is ultimately in my opinion far more successful as a Halloween film than as a Christmas film. Yet it was released only shortly before Halloween. It opened in selected theaters in mid-October and was widely released on October 29. Thus, any commercial potential as a Halloween event was extremely truncated, yet its content is more suited to that holiday than to Christmas. The feel of the film is dark and gruesome in the style that director Tim Burton (Batman, Edward Scissorshands) is well known for. Most of the action takes place in Halloweenland, as Jack Skellington finds himself suffering from ennui. It seems that in Halloweenland it is always Halloween, and Jack has gotten bored. But one day in the forest Jack finds the doorways to other lands: trees, one with a heart, one with an egg, one with a shamrock, and one with a decorated evergreen for Christmas. Jack enters this land, and discovers a place full of song and joy and gift-giving. Determining that this was just what Halloweenland needs, Skellington concocts a plan to bring Christmas to Halloweenland. He kidnaps Santa and takes his place delivering gifts on Christmas Eve. He cannot transcend being the creature he is, however: a product of, a manifestation of, Halloween. So while trying his mightiest to do the right thing, the toys he delivers are malevolent, deadly. Eventually, Santa Claus, who is being tortured back in Halloweenland, escapes and sets things aright.

The Nightmare Before Christmas contains references and allusions to several other well-known Christmas narratives. When Skellington delivers presents, he hitches his ghostly dog to a skeletal sleigh. The

dog has a glowing orange pumpkin nose in a Halloween translation of
the Rudolph story. Similarly, throughout the film (and in the numerous print editions) we can find allusions to *The Grinch Who Stole
Christmas* and "A Visit from St. Nicholas" ("The Night Before Christmas")—clearly, the title of the film is a pun on this famous first line of
Clement C. Moore. Also, there is a great deal of death imagery
throughout, most notably gravestones and graveyards. One might
identify rebirth symbolism juxtaposed with these icons of death without straining credulity too far. Generally through the film's allusions
to other well-known Christmas stories, its self-awareness is apparent
throughout and calls attention to itself. In this regard the film is
postmodern in its sensibilities.

The very juxtaposition of Halloween and Christmas is perhaps the
most foregrounded feature of the film. Judging from personal conver-
sations and the publicity surrounding the release of the film, the
bringing together of the two sets of symbolic codes seemed culturally
wrong to many people. Halloween may feature death imagery in real
life, followed in time by sacred images of newborn life, and these may
correspond exceedingly well with the seasonal occurrences during
which they take place, but they do not appear to naturally fit together
in a single filmic narrative. Burton pointed out that he saw this same
jarring juxtaposition in department stores every fall: on one aisle was
Halloween merchandise, and there on the next, Christmas materials.
What Burton says is true, and it is interesting to think of *The Nightmare Before Christmas* as reflecting that commercial reality. Ironically,
the narrative ultimately reinforces the incompatibility of Halloween
and Christmas.

The film can be read in many ways, of course. Some see the moral
as a rather disturbing reinforcement of the status quo. Jack
Skellington belongs where he is, and that's that. Any attempt to
change and try new things is met with disaster. Other people suggest
an alternative reading, wherein people (and skeletons) need to be
aware of their own greatest abilities, to accept what they do best
and to celebrate it. Jack Skellington is very good at what he does,

being the king of Halloweenland. In this view, the film is about self-recognition, self-acceptance, and self-respect.

But does it work as a holiday film? If so, which holiday? When the film was released in the autumn of 1993, the graphic image most commonly associated with the advertising depicted a solitary Jack Skellington standing atop a snowbank that resembled a cresting ocean wave. Below him is a field of pumpkins, each carved as a jack-o'-lantern, each face illuminated. The snow is the only remotely non-Halloween symbol, and it is not Christmas-oriented but merely seasonal, nor is it particularly identifiable. As I stated, the film is somewhat of an anomaly in that it combines two symbolic sets that are not usually combined, and rather than achieve a synthesis of the two it validates their mutual exclusivity. When the film was released as a home video, however, the accompanying advertising poster featured a Christmas scene. Furthermore, this was not a Skellington-delivering-deadly-snakes-and-explosive-toys scene, as would have been in keeping with the general tone of the film, but rather a scene from the visit to Christmas Town. The images are clearly Christmas icons, and happy smiling children are depicted dancing at Santa's feet. Clearly the intention was to pitch the film in an entirely different manner, as a more traditional, warm-hearted Christmas movie, an animated feature suitable for all ages.

I saw the movie with my three children, aged three, four, and six at the time. I squirmed as they were exposed to scenes of maggots crawling out of people's skulls and other equally disgusting, horrific images. I believe fully that the film is too dark and too strong for children that age. After it was over, though, they all said they liked it, and seemed unscathed by the images that so bothered me. The one important exception was my four-year-old, Will, who was very disturbed by the perverted Santa sequence and needed reassurance on that score. He repeatedly asked me about the deadly Christmas gifts of Jack Skellington, and did not grasp the reassurance provided in the film that Santa had undone the harm and given real gifts. I was not able to interpret the film through the eyes of a child. Will found *The*

Nightmare Before Christmas disturbing, but not in the way I had expected.

Christmas Narratives, Folk and Popular

Narrative is central to both the sacred and secular rituals of the
Christmas season. The birth of Jesus is the basis for the sacred observance of Christmas Day; the story is ritually retold in church every
year. The same is true for the Circumcision, January 1, and the
Epiphany (the arrival of the magi to adore the holy baby), on January 6, Twelfth Night. These narratives are found in sacred Christian
scripture and are recounted during holy rituals. Secular stories are
important at this time as well, and many of them are broadcast on the
popular media. From children's cartoons to theatrical dramas, narratives concerning the holiday provide some of the pleasures of the season. In the United States, many of us, both children and adults, enjoy
watching *How the Grinch Stole Christmas* or *A Charlie Brown Christmas*
on television; or we go to the movie theater to see the latest Christmas release. Charles Dickens's *A Christmas Carol* is very popular
throughout this period; it is available in print, film, video, and stage
presentations, having been interpreted and reinterpreted in numbers
almost beyond count (see Davis 1990).

Not surprisingly, seasonal narratives have been important components of folk celebrations as well. One such form of narrative is the
folk drama or play. Traditionally in Europe, the British Isles, Ireland,
and North America, the celebration of Christmas was accompanied
with mumming (from the Danish word *mumme,* to mask). Christmas
mumming, which is still found in certain areas, consists of groups of
men in disguise who troop from household to household, where they
expect or demand gifts of food and drink in return for a performance
of a traditional drama or skit. While the term can be used broadly to
refer to any group of roaming performers who beg or demand favors,
more specifically it refers to Northern European, Anglo, and Irish traditional practices. Both of the American customs of Christmas carol-

ing and Halloween trick-or-treating are related to these practices.
These Northern European, English, and Irish folk dramas are humorous, boisterous enactments that center on the slaying and resurrection of one of the characters. The plays, and the custom, appear to be
pre-Christian in origin. Among the *dramatis personae* for instance, is
often a Wild Man, who is most likely a nature divinity of some kind,
included along with historical and legendary figures like St. George,
the patron saint of England, or St. Patrick in Ireland. Scholars have
long believed that these mummers' plays are a kind of nature allegory
of the death and rebirth of the sun, which accounts for these plays
being performed around the time of the winter solstice (see, for example, Brody 1969; Halpert and Story 1969; and Glassie 1975).

Brody, in his study, examines the hero-combat and the death-res-
urrection motifs using a British text that he considers representative,
the Netley Abbey Mummers' Play. I would like to refer to some of his
examples to both give a sense of what the plays are like, and to high-
light some features of them that I find interesting, especially when we
examine them alongside some of the popular narratives associated
with Christmas today. Mummers' plays usually have a good number
of characters, whose number and identity vary greatly from place
to place and from time to time. In this text, the play begins with a
rhyme from the First Christmas Boy, who in turn introduces Father
Christmas.

> In comes I, old Father Christmas
>
> Welcome or welcome not,
>
> I hope old Father Christmas
>
> Will never be forgot.

Other characters enter as they are introduced, including the Turkey Snipe or Turkish Knight, and King George. George eventually
challenges the Turkey Snipe:

> Pull out your purse and pay,
>
> Pull out your sword and fight.

> Satisfaction I will have
>
> Before I leave this night

The Turkey Snipe responds:

> No purse will I pull out,
>
> No money will I pay,
>
> But my sword I will draw out
>
> And have satisfaction of thee this day.
>
> Battle, battle, battle I will call,
>
> And see which on the ground shall fall.

King George then says:

> Battle, battle, I will cry,
>
> To see which on the ground shall lie.

At this point, the Turkish Knight is wounded and falls. He is lamented by Father Christmas:

> Horrible, terrible, what hast thou done?
>
> Thou has killed my only dearly beloved son
>
> Is there a doctor to be found
>
> To cure him of his deep and deadly wound?

The doctor, a comical figure, takes the stage, and cures the fallen knight. According to Brody, the resurrection is "the most perfunctory part of the cure section of the play. After the doctor has administered his medicine, the victim simply revives" (59).

Henry Glassie's 1975 study of Christmas mumming in the Ballymenone district of Northern Ireland, *All Silver and No Brass,* provides an interesting comparison to the above material. Although the mumming was no longer performed in this area at the time of his research, Glassie interviewed elderly people who remembered the plays and had performed in them. The following selections are taken from

the longer reminiscence of Peter Boyle, as told to and recorded by
Glassie. The play described features St. Patrick in search of Prince
George:

> Here comes I Saint Patrick.
>
> "And the reason I came,
>
> I'm in search of that bully
>
> Prince George is his name.
>
> And if I do find him,
>
> I'll tell you no lie,
>
> I'll hack him to pieces as small as a fly.
>
> And throw 'im to the Devil for a Christmas pie."

Patrick then encounters Oliver Cromwell:

> "I swear, by George, you lie, sir."

> "Pull out your purse and pay, sir."

> "I'll run my rapier through your side,
>
> and make you die away, sir."

Patrick falls and a doctor is called in, who recites a comic monologue
regarding his medicaments, ending with "Rise up dead man and fight
again." Mr. Boyle then says, "So then the dead man rises up and that's
that." (1975, 40–44). He goes on to describe the concluding sections
of the play.

Scholarship on Christmas mumming, with some more recent exceptions, has tended to focus on the death-rebirth motif found in the
performances and to link them to the solar and seasonal year. That is,
because the plays were performed around the time of the winter solstice, the day of the least amount of daylight of the year and the point
after which the amount of daylight increases for six months, the death

of the hero figure and his rebirth was taken as a metaphorical allusion
to the death and rebirth of the sun. Related to this is the idea that the
death-rebirth scene is also related to the death of winter and the rebirth of spring. Richard Bauman has said that Christmas mumming
was "all but made to order" for nineteenth-century antiquarians and
twentieth-century survivalists. "The antiquity of the institution was
well documented, its seasonal significance was unquestionable, and its
ritual nature apparently obvious. Accordingly, the literature on
mumming abounds with references to fertility gods, saturnalia, and
death and resurrection, all focused backwards on the roots of the
custom in dim antiquity" (Bauman 1972, 229). Glassie has balanced
these Frazerian excesses with the more commonsense suggestion
that "if we ignore the old assumption of degeneration, and replace the
idea of magical causation with one of logical relation and metaphoric
involvement, the drama's connection to the death of one year and the
birth of another could be worth exploration" (1975, 103).

Just as folklorists have turned their orientation from speculation
over origins in a long-vanished past to a social and symbolic consideration of such materials among people for whom mumming is a personally experienced reality, I would like to move to a discussion of
popular Christmas narratives in terms of their social use in contemporary society before commenting further on the mummers' plays.
Turning first to Charles Dickens's novel A Christmas Carol, it has been
documented that this story has been presented at Christmastime, in
many different media, both in Great Britain and the United States virtually every year since it was first published in 1846 (Davis 1990).

A Christmas Carol was a popular success upon its publication. Very
quickly it spawned scores of imitations, both theatrical and printed.
Throughout his lifetime, Dickens himself gave public readings of it;
since his death, the Carol has appeared in numerous film and television adaptations. Several silent film versions of it were made as early
as 1910 (Davis 1990). The story of the miserly old man who, through
the agencies of the spirits of Christmas Past, Present, and Future, witnesses his own death and is reborn a new man on Christmas Day has
become a part of the Christmas celebration itself. Scrooge has been

portrayed by Henry Winkler, George C. Scott, Alistaire Sim, Albert
Finney, and Scrooge McDuck (among many, many others). The
American holiday season is marked by the broadcasting of one or another of the many film and television versions of the *Carol;* it is in this
respect that I consider it a popular form that has itself become traditional to the holiday it describes.

The same can be said of certain other popular narratives that appear on film, most notably, the famous Frank Capra film *It's a Wonderful Life* (1946). Although this story has not been reinterpreted as often
as the *Carol,* it has been said with only a little exaggeration that between Thanksgiving, in late November, and New Year's Day there is
not a moment in the day when *It's a Wonderful Life* is not playing
somewhere in the United States. Interestingly, this film too is about a
desperate man who witnesses his own death, only to be reborn and
renewed on Christmas Day. Other films, such as the more recent and
less successful Disney effort, *One Magic Christmas* (1985), center on
the same death and rebirth motif, and the list can easily be extended.

Dickens wrote an instant classic, but did he invent the Christmas
ghost story? We know he based some of his ideas on the nineteenth-
century custom of telling ghost stories on Christmas Eve. As in the
case of the mummers' plays, the relationship of the ghostly to Christmas festivities owes a great deal to the positioning of Christmas at
the time of the winter solstice, after which the amount of daylight increases daily, and to the turning of the calendrical year as well. As we
have seen, such turning points, whether solar or calendrical, are often
accompanied by belief in supernatural activity.

Just as I selected short portions of the mummers' plays for examples, I would like to describe certain scenes in three Christmas
movies as examples of some typical motifs found in Christmas films.
There is a great deal of mutual influence here; *A Christmas Carol* is ar-
guably the model for each film I will describe. However, the themes
contained in these and other Christmas films are not restricted to the
Carol, and in fact predate it, even as we demonstrate that the scenes
concerning death and rebirth in these films are similar in small details
as well as in overall themes. I will begin with *It's a Wonderful Life.*

This film stars Jimmy Stewart as George Bailey, a hardworking, decent man who lives his life in the town of Bedford Falls. We see him first as a boy, then as a young man. We follow his biography as he grows, marries, has children, and wins the respect of his friends and neighbors. Although a good man, George has always wanted to go to college, travel, see the world, and have adventures, but his sense of decency has kept him home to take care of one responsibility or another. In this regard, he is frustrated. Then his life begins to unravel, through a series of unfortunate mishaps and deliberate ill will. Eventually he is forced to beg his archrival for a loan, an act that is to him akin to selling one's soul to the devil. By this point in the film, George has hit bottom. He is mean and short-tempered with his family and disgusted with himself. On Christmas Eve, he visits the local bar and begins to drink. "Oh God," he whispers, "I'm not a praying man. But I'm at the end of my rope. Give me a sign." Just then the man to his left recognizes him as the person who in a fit of rage insulted his wife, and punches George in the face, knocking him to the ground. "That's what I get for praying," says George.

He decides to kill himself. Staggering from the bar he makes his way to a bridge overlooking a rushing river. Although he does not yet know it, his guardian angel, named Clarence, is also on the bridge. As Bailey looks at the swirling waters and prepares to jump, saying the world would have been a better place had he never been born, a splash is seen in the river. Clarence jumped first. Bailey immediately dives in and saves him. Perhaps this is the first sign of Bailey's redemption, that even at the hour of his despair, he was willing to put someone else's life ahead of his.

Clarence explains that he is an angel, and George of course does not believe him. Nevertheless, Clarence grants George his wish that he was never born, then takes him on a tour of the town to demonstrate to George just what a difference his life had in fact made.

Everything is different, including the town itself. It is now called Pottersville, after his archenemy who obviously controls it. Pottersville is a cheap, tawdry place of night joints, neon lights, gambling, and prostitution. His friends are tough and cynical; their lives are miserable. In one scene, Clarence brings George to a graveyard where he sees the grave of his younger brother, whom he had once saved from drowning in an ice-skating accident as a child. George bends over the grave and wipes the snow off the stone to reveal the name Bailey. He rejects the idea of his brother's death. "My brother was a hero! He saved the lives of the 86th Airborne in the war!" Clarence responds: "All those men died in the war because your brother wasn't there to save them, because you weren't there to save him when he fell in the ice!"

George then demands to know what happened to his wife. After some hesitation, Clarence shows him: she is unmarried and working as a librarian. In what is an otherwise excellent film, this section is badly dated. His wife, played by Donna Reed, is portrayed as a stereotypical "old maid," wearing a shawl and a cap, her hair tied back in a severe fashion. The message is that a woman remaining unmarried and having a career of her own—especially as a librarian—is self-evidently a bad thing. It is the most "wrong" thing about Pottersville; it is what most needs to be fixed by the return of George. Seeing his beloved Mary this way breaks George. Sobbing frantically, he returns to the bridge and cries for help. "Get me back, Clarence, get me back. I want to live! I want to live!" he calls out, over and over. When Bert the police officer drives up to the bridge, George assumes he is still in the reality in which he does not exist, but when it becomes apparent that he is "back," he gives the astonished police officer a great hug. From there George returns home, full of joy and love for his family, and for life itself. Meanwhile, Mary has recruited the townspeople, who together help George with the financial difficulties that had led to his despair. His daughter leads everyone in a Christmas song. It is Christmas Eve, and the film ends with a joyous celebration of community.

These scenes are at the heart of this particular film. They also echo scenes of previous movies and other Christmas stories. For instance, how many of the *Christmas Carol* adaptations have depicted Scrooge reading his own name on a tombstone? It is one of the central scenes of the story. George Bailey is not a Scrooge figure, and he does not see his own death exactly, but rather, he sees what life would have been like if he had never been born. Never having been born, he cannot have died. However, he does view a tombstone and confronts the name Bailey engraved in it. This scene is very dramatic, and I believe it is meant to suggest, or at least substitute for, George's seeing his own gravestone. Also, when George decides he wants to rescind his wish for nonexistence, it is with the cry "I want to live! I want to live!"

There are other, even more specific parallels among the scenes I have recounted and those of other Christmas films. Although we cannot possibly survey the many, many adaptations of A Christmas Carol, an investigation of one recent version is instructive. Scrooged (1988), stars comedian Bill Murray as Francis Xavier Cross, a television producer who is putting on a production of A Christmas Carol for the Christmas television season. Cross is the Scrooge figure in the film, and his story is overtly based on Dickens's account of Scrooge. For instance, while in the Carol Scrooge witnessed a Christmas ball at his nephew's, Cross sees a party at his brother's, where the game is Trivial Pursuit. The film generally follows the narrative of the Carol; Cross has had his heart hardened toward Christmas, due largely to a bad childhood. Like Scrooge, he is visited upon by three spirits of Christmas, past, present, and yet-to-come.

In the Christmas-yet-to-come scene, Cross is shown a large room, empty except for a preacher, his sister-in-law, and a coffin that stands before a raging furnace. He assumes his brother has died, but then his brother enters the room. He begins to realize that the coffin is his own. He walks to the front of the casket and reads his name on it. As the coffin starts to slide into the flames, Cross tries to hold it back. "Help me!" he says. "I don't want to burn!" Suddenly he is inside the coffin. Flames engulf him. "I want to live!" he screams like Bailey, "I want to live!" Just as suddenly, he is inside an elevator, still pounding on the opening doors. "I'm alive! I'm alive! Holy shit!" The "Hallelujah" Chorus comes up on the soundtrack. Cross is delirious with excitement and joy. He falls before an image of the sun on the wall and exclaims, "Look! The sun!" Behind him appears a character carrying a rifle, intent on taking his life. Still enraptured with the joy of being

alive, Cross turns, pushes aside the weapon and embraces his potential killer. "I'm the Woodstock baby!" he cries. Cross's conversion is
real, and from this point he spreads his cheer. The film continues to
deliberately follow *A Christmas Carol* as, in its final scene, the film's
Tiny Tim, a mute boy named Calvin, miraculously speaks, saying,
"God bless us, everyone."

Both George Bailey and Frank Cross embrace men armed with
guns immediately upon their rebirth. Like Ebenezer Scrooge and
George Bailey, Frank Cross reads his own name on his grave/coffin.
Like them, he is reborn: the mention of the Woodstock baby is a reference to a baby that was reported to have been born during the
Woodstock Music Festival of 1969. It is significant that Murray's character upon rebirth identified himself with both the sun and a newborn
baby as did Scrooge in the original, recalling imagery reminiscent of
both Christmas and the winter solstice, and recalling the interpretations of the mummers' plays as solar allegories. Certainly the death
and rebirth motifs are in operation here as well.

In 1985, Disney Productions released a film called *One Magic Christmas.* Although not as commercially successful as the others we have
looked at, the film has enjoyed continual, uninterrupted, year-round
shelf life in my local video rental store. *One Magic Christmas* combines
elements of both *A Christmas Carol* and *It's a Wonderful Life* with a
touch of *Miracle on 34th Street* (1947) thrown in as well. The protagonist who has had her heart hardened against Christmas in this film, a
woman this time, is named Ginny Grainger. As in *Wonderful Life,* an
angel has been assigned to help her find the "Christmas spirit." Her
younger child, a girl, believes in Christmas generally and in Santa
Claus particularly. Jack, her husband, is an incurable romantic, fond of
the season, as is her older child, a son. At first it seems that Ginny
resents Christmas simply because her family has little money. She
works for a difficult supervisor at a grocery store; her husband has
been laid off his job. The children expect lots of presents that Ginny
feels they simply cannot afford. Her daughter asks her to mail a letter
to Santa Claus that she has written, but Ginny merely puts it in a
drawer.

One night, walking with her husband, Ginny questions the value
and meaning of life. "What good is it?" she asks.

"Why, to take walks on nights like these," Jack answers. "To see
the stars in the sky."

"That reminds me of a song I used to sing when I was a little girl,"
she responds, and begins singing "And we're lost out here in the
stars," from a song by Maxwell Anderson and Kurt Weill called "Lost
in the Stars." The choice of this song at this point in the movie gains
in significance when one knows the song in its entirety. The song tells
the story of a little star that gets lost, so God promises to watch over
it in the future. The lyrics of the song that immediately precede what
we hear in the film are as follows:

> But I've been walking through the night and
> 　the day
> Till my eyes get weary and my head turns gray.
> And sometimes it seems maybe God's gone
> 　away,
> forgetting the promise that we heard Him say
> and we're lost out here in the stars.

("Lost in the Stars," by Maxwell Anderson and Kurt Weill, © 1944,
1946 [copyrights renewed] TRO Hampshire House Publishing
Corp. & Chappell & Co. All rights reserved. Used by permission.
Warner Bros. Publications U.S. Inc., Miami, Fla. 33014)

In a sense, then, the song's words exactly parallel Jimmy Stewart's
prayer and declaration of despair immediately preceding his decision
to kill himself. God has apparently abandoned them both. Considering
what happens next in One Magic Christmas, we see that the song is
used at the same point in the structure of the film, as well. In both
cases the motif is a desperate beseeching of the almighty followed by
a major plot development concerning death and oblivion.

"If you're trying to cheer me up, you're doing a lousy job of it,"
Jack replies upon hearing his wife sing. "I'm going for one more turn

around the block." With that, he walks away by himself. Ginny walks
to the nearby mailbox. Gideon, the angel, a rather frightening figure
dressed in black, startles her.

"Mailing letters to the North Pole?" he asks.

"I think I'm a little old for the North Pole," she replies.

"You don't sound like you have much Christmas spirit."

"Do I know you?"

"No."

"No, I didn't think so. No, no, I don't have much Christmas spirit."
Ginny turns and walks away.

"But you should, you know. That's too bad." Surprised at this
stranger's impertinence, Ginny turns around. Gideon is nowhere to
be seen. Then, all the Christmas lights in the neighborhood start going
off, frighteningly. Ginny returns home, and life, apparently, goes on.

Things go from bad to worse. The next day the family drives into
town. Jack goes to the bank, interrupting a robbery in progress. He
tries to calm the robber but is shot. Ginny rushes to the bank, cradles
her fallen husband, only to find that he is dead. The robber, meanwhile, steals her car and kidnaps her children. Ginny chases him in
another automobile, until the robber crashes into a river. Though we
see Gideon rescue the children, for a while Ginny thinks her entire
family has been lost.

Gideon has struck up a friendship with the younger child, who believes him to be who he claims to be. He arranges for her to travel to
the North Pole to meet Santa Claus. There, Santa discovers a letter
that Ginny had sent to him when she was a little girl. He had mis-
placed it all these years. So we learn that Ginny's cynicism began at a
tender age, when Santa never answered her letter. No wonder she is
reluctant to mail her daughter's letter! She wants to spare her the
hurt of finding out there is no Santa Claus. In this movie, however,
there *is* a Santa Claus. Returning home, her daughter tells her brother
of her adventure, but he does not believe her. Neither, of course,
does Ginny, but in a moment of tender feelings, decides to mail her
daughter's letter. Once again, Gideon is standing by the mailbox.
Based on things her daughter has told her, Ginny has guessed that he

must be Gideon, and calls him so by name. She mails the letter and smiles. Suddenly, the Christmas lights turn on, and in the distance she hears whistling. She hardly dares think it, but who should be coming along but her husband Jack! She embraces him. "You're alive! You're alive!" Jack is bemused. "Of course I'm alive, honey. Don't you remember singing that little song to me just a few minutes ago?"

Both this scene and the miracle it depicts are strongly reminiscent of *It's a Wonderful Life.* There is still another miracle left in the film, however. On Christmas Eve, the two children, both still awake, hear thumping on the rooftop. "Santa Claus?" asks the older boy. "Santa Claus," says the younger girl. Ginny hears noises too, and comes downstairs to investigate. She sees Santa Claus. Santa waves to her. Ginny's face registers first astonishment, then joy, as the movie ends. The change of heart that enabled Ginny to mail her daughter's letter, though she still did not herself believe in Santa Claus, indicated an acceptance of the "Christmas spirit," which was sufficient to warrant the return of her husband to life. As a sort of additional reward, she is allowed to see Santa, to know that he really does exist.

Like George Bailey, Ginny questioned the meaning of life itself immediately prior to the initiation of supernatural events. Although it is her husband who, like Scrooge and George Bailey, dies and returns, the story focuses on Ginny's *spiritual* rebirth. She is the Scrooge figure in this movie. Even the name of the character—Ginny—is significant. Her full name would be Virginia, presumably, echoing the famous "Yes, Virginia, there is a Santa Claus" editorial response to a little girl's letter decades ago. Since the plot of the film culminates in the lead character's coming to accept the reality of Santa Claus, we can assume that the choice of name is no accident. Just as the song "Lost in the Stars" was carefully selected for its lyric content, so does the name Ginny carry with it associations with other Christmas traditions. Knowledge of these associations adds depth and meaning to the film.

The three films we have discussed all feature a death and rebirth, but if we extend the concept more broadly to include the kind of spiritual rebirth we see with Ginny, then other Christmas narratives such as *Miracle on 34th Street* and *How the Grinch Stole Christmas* also feature this theme. In the films examined above, death and rebirth are a metaphor for transformation. It is interesting that so many of our Christmas stories today feature the death and rebirth, in one way or another, of the protagonists, much as there was a death and resurrection of the central characters of the mummers' plays.

I want to draw attention to the extension of the death and rebirth motif into our era in the plots of the popular narratives described above. I recognize the enormous social, cultural, and contextual differences between British and Irish mummers' plays that have not been performed for almost a century and the electronic mass media of contemporary America. In no way am I seeking to equate the two, or imply a causal connection between them. Rather, I am suggesting that the same dichotomies of old year and new year, waning light and waxing light, shorter and longer days, death and rebirth, old and young and so forth, that informed the winter narratives of old are addressed today in films and television programs such as *A Christmas Carol* and *It's a Wonderful Life*.

The connection of Christmas with death is present in the numerous murder mysteries set at this time of year as well, and these may be related to this larger theme. Also in this regard, I have become aware of interesting European parallels in Northern Ireland and in Norway. In both cases, I learned of folk narratives—legends—that are associated with Christmas, and popular television programs that are regularly broadcast at Christmastime. In both cases, the legends differed markedly in tone from the television programs, but in all cases, the stories dealt with Christmas ghosts and the confrontation with death prior to awakening to glorious life on Christmas Day.

It may be worth pointing out that the dichotomies referred to above are also manifested in the figures of old men and young boys— babies—paired iconographically throughout this season. Certainly the figures of the old year as an Old Man and the New Year as a baby are examples; so perhaps are Santa Claus—who is, at least in part, an "old man winter" figure—and the Baby Jesus (again, I recognize that the social meanings of these figures are drastically different). Similarly, in the *Carol*, Ebenezer Scrooge is paired with Tiny Tim.

When I say that I recognize vast differences in the narratives along all the performative and social parameters, I mean it. While they can be compared broadly, and interestingly, according to the death-rebirth motif and the calendrical time frame of winter–Christmas–New Year (and even Halloween, an old New Year marker in some places), do we feel comfortable with this? When I suggest that a Bill Murray movie, or an old Jimmy Stewart film run on television, con-tains solar, seasonal, or spiritual symbolism, does it ring true? Do we ever actually think of these things when we watch these? We can deconstruct a text by examining the full lyrics to a brief snatch of song used in a film, or by relating an important character's name to a famous incident, but this in no way ensures that people interpret the films in these ways.

If we feel uncomfortable with this kind of interpretation of materi-als that we ourselves are involved with, this suggests several things. First and most obvious is that we need the ethnographic data referred to above to make a more informed analysis. Second, however, I feel that the kinds of meanings I am talking about tend to be unarticulated, so the fact that they may sound far-fetched to some people when they first hear them does not necessarily rule out the possibility that there may be some truth to them. A third point worth making here, however, has to do more with the mummers' plays I compared them with. When talking about the plays of a past time, we do not object to these kinds of statements. I wonder, though, if they would not have seemed equally outlandish to the participants and audiences of the plays? A comparison of the English and Irish mummers' play texts that were excerpted above reveal obvious but profound differences. In the English text, St. George, the patron saint of England, slays a Turkish Knight. In the Irish play, the patron saint of Ireland has set off to kill St. George. He is met and challenged by Oliver Cromwell, who not only represents England, but also was the great enemy of Roman Catholicism as well. Clearly, an Irish audience would read political content in these performances. In a similar way, when *It's a Wonderful Life* is viewed today, the scene that depicts Bailey's wife as an unmarried librarian, presenting this stereotypically as the worst of all possible fates, causes contemporary audiences to groan. In its day, however, audiences presumably did not react this way. Although we may not recognize them, social and political messages are also contained in modern films. In our romantic views of the folk societies of the past, we like to believe that people lived in some kind of harmony with nature and the cosmos. In reality, those mumming performances were just as politically loaded as the movies today. Would the people then have been any more cognizant of the presumed solar symbolism than we are? To reduce either the old plays or the modern films to seasonal, solar symbolism alone is to do them a disservice.

It is true that *It's a Wonderful Life* owes at least some of its inspiration to Dickens's *A Christmas Carol.* Dickens owes at least some of his inspiration to the Victorian tradition of telling ghost stories at Christmas. This tradition owes at least some of its inspiration to the fact that Christmas represents a magical time, a transitional time, when the supernatural can and does occur. Christmas owes at least some of this sense of magic to the transitional nature of the event: it occurs near the winter solstice and is connected to the ending of one year and the beginning of another. The narrative plots of our most successful and recent Christmas stories involve a death and rebirth motif as a central plot element, with an emphasis on the essential transformation of the character.

But that is not enough. Not every story becomes an almost ritualistic viewing experience. *It's a Wonderful Life* was not originally released widely until after Christmas, and, while not unsuccessful, it was not a runaway hit. In recent years, with the proliferation of television stations, due to the growth of the cable industry and the resultant need for product, along with the availability of *It's a Wonderful Life* as it entered the public domain, the film has become a staple of December television programming. The very fact that the film was in the public domain, meaning it could be broadcast without paying royalties to anyone, is enough to account for the repeated broadcasts of this movie during the Christmas season. Still, the plot elements described above lend the film a kind of relevance to the season on several different levels: solar, seasonal, metaphoric, and symbolic, which in turn provide the potential for *It's a Wonderful Life* to become a contemporary Christmas classic.

It is valid to note the death and rebirth symbolism and its connection with the solstice and the turning of the year. It is also worth pointing out that the stories I am referring to tend to parallel the Christian Nativity story and emphasize Christian values without actually referring to Christianity. In this regard, what I find interesting in many Christmas films is how Santa Claus is treated. Santa does not appear in *A Christmas Carol,* of course, nor in *It's a Wonderful Life.* But there are a great many movies in which the conversion miracle hinges on the acceptance of the reality of Santa Claus.

Generally, Santa is portrayed in popular Christmas narratives, especially films, as a figure who really exists. Through the course of the story, a doubting adult is converted. Interestingly, it is almost blasphemous to admit in Christian American society that in truth, there is no Santa Claus. From "Yes, Virginia, there is a Santa Claus" through *Miracle on 34th Street,* Santa is a figure who, having been invented, is periodically reaffirmed.

In one way, he is reinvented as social conditions change. Lévi-Strauss has suggested that Santa, or rather, Father Christmas, represents the transformation of the Lord of Misrule associated with inversive midwinter festivities into a "symbol of maturity which is favorably disposed toward youth" (Lévi-Strauss 1993 [1952] in Miller, ed. 1993, 48). Increasingly, efforts are made to distance him from the Christian St. Nicholas. For instance, *Santa Claus: The Movie* provides an entirely non-Christian (some would say pagan) origin for him, as did L. Frank Baum's *The Life and Adventures of Santa Claus* before that ([1879] 1976). Having belief periodically reaffirmed through retelling of certain narratives sounds similar to the ritual telling of mythic narratives in other societies, but this brings us back to the same prob-

lems we encountered when we compared the films with the mummers' plays as solstice rituals. It is too simplistic and blurs important
differences in meanings, contexts, and social usages. Rather, the most
we can reasonably and responsibly say is that an analogy exists.

What is the point of insisting in so many of these movies that Santa
Claus really does exist? The protagonist of One Magic Christmas has an
experience reminiscent of It's a Wonderful Life in which her husband
dies, but when she finally opens her heart to the Christmas spirit, the
entire episode is erased. Yet, after this, she sees Santa Claus delivering toys and presents in her living room. Also her older son, who has
outgrown his belief, hears Santa on the rooftop and is reconvinced. In
the 1990 movie Prancer, a deer is thought by a child to be Santa's
reindeer. At the end of the film the deer disappears, apparently having
fallen off a cliff to its death. The little girl's father, the character whose
heart was, Scrooge-like, hardened to Christmas, has by now experienced his conversion, his rebirth and renewal. But the question of
Prancer's real identity remains. And what should we see silhouetted
by the moon but Santa and his reindeer flying through the sky? The
final scene of Miracle on 34th Street, with Kris Kringle's cane left in the
dream house of the now-transformed mother who did not believe in
Christmas, strongly implies a real miracle by the real Santa Claus.

Why is so much effort made to affirm the existence of a figure who
does not, in reality, exist? About whose existence in fact there is no
debate? The films, it will be said, are aimed at children, as is the Santa
Claus mythology. The films only add to the child's sense of wonder.
Nevertheless, these films are also aimed at adults; certainly Miracle on
34th Street would be difficult for a youngster to sustain interest in. My
experience watching Prancer in a theater full of youngsters is that it
was over the heads of, and too dark a film for, children below the age
of seven; the same can be said for One Magic Christmas, and others as
well. These films feature adults who, like the adults in the audience,
provide Christmas for youngsters, who pass on the Santa Claus legends and traditions. It is they who find, through the course of the
film, that Santa really does exist.

For an adult to believe in Santa Claus is in a sense a return to childhood because belief in Santa Claus is the domain of the very young. Belief in Santa is a sign of children's unspoiled ability to have faith. To believe again is to return to a childlike state of being in which one believes uncritically in the existence or at least the possibility of magic, and a return to a quality of being that, in believing, has access to this magic. The Christian parallel, that unless one becomes as a little child one shall not enter the kingdom of heaven, is an indication that the belief in childhood as a time of innocence and faith is very deep in our culture. It also indicates the fundamentally Christian nature of supposedly secular Christmas entertainments. In the Christmas movies, by becoming like a little child, one goes to the North Pole, or sees Santa Claus, or at least enters into the Edenic paradise of a reconciled loving family relationship.

Perhaps the answer has something to do with the old man–baby dichotomy I referred to above, and the transformation of the Christmas story from the Jesus nativity narrative to the Santa Claus myth. Santa implies children; believing in one half of the dichotomy implies the validity of the other half. Also, if Santa is in part an iconographic representation of winter, then to that extent he is real; that is, what he represents is certainly real. If he is an iconographic representation of the humane (but not necessarily Christian) values of Christmas, these are at least sometimes real. Insistence in the belief in Santa Claus is a statement of faith in the reality and value of these virtues. To believe in Santa Claus is to believe in what he stands for. To believe in a symbol is to believe in what the symbol represents in all its many associations (see Turner 1967). Thus, one believes in the flag, one believes in the cross, and one believes in Santa Claus. This is the point of the famous editorial answer to Virginia's question. Further: Santa's great age implies youth and rejuvenation, paired iconographically with youth. He lives, significantly, in a land of endless winter— the North Pole, but he visits us only in December, near, it must be again pointed out, the winter solstice. He is winter personified, but he is benevolent, paternal. His winter promises spring. This is in contrast to European Santas, St. Nicks, and other midwinter gift-bringers like the Italian Befana, whose function is to punish as well as reward. In the United States, Santa has been said to leave a lump of coal in the stockings of bad children, or soot and cinders in the United Kingdom, but even this aspect of his story is diminishing.

Belk (1993) sees Santa as a personification of consumerism, which in the person of Santa becomes the medium of celebration of family and community. Santa's existence is intimately linked with childhood. Interestingly, the social dynamics having to do with separation of church and state, and questions having to do with the degree to which Christmas is a specifically religious, Christian holiday as opposed to a national secular holiday have led to a direct linking by some of Santa with the image of the sacred Baby Jesus, thus rendering more explicit the old man–baby dichotomy. In the films, no matter how specifically they insist on the literal reality of Santa Claus, the figure is nevertheless allegorical of the goodwill and great joy of the Christmas season, and even the glad tidings of the biblical accounts.

The supernatural can occur at this time of year in all probability because of the transitional nature of the period: winter solstice, midwinter, new year. But the specific supernatural incursions into everyday life, from Scrooge through ghost stories told by firelight to the appearance in our world of an ageless, magic man we ourselves invented and dare believe in only as children, all reaffirm cultural values and economic and social life. Despite its festive, licentious aspects (eating, drinking, making merry) Christmas is a festival that today chiefly promotes socially cohesive values, perhaps none more so than the value of children and the need to attend to our relationship with them. The putative secular elements and values of Christmas closely adumbrate Christian themes and values. The sacred image at this time is not only the baby Jesus but also his parents and in decreasing importance, his friends and admirers, spread out in decreasing degree of relationship from the baby in the crèche scenes. Paralleling this, Santa often poses for photographs with our children on his knee. There is an analogy here, having to do not only with a sacred child, but with children as sacred and also with parental relationships to them. Is it too much to say that belief in Santa Claus equals belief in the nuclear family; specifically, a nuclear family rooted in a capitalistic lifestyle?

Watch *Miracle on 34th Street* again, with this in mind; or *Prancer,* with its reconciliation of father and daughter, or 1990's *Home Alone,* or 1991's *All I Want for Christmas.* Of course, Santa himself is married: Mrs. Claus is now a general part of the Santa iconography. And at least one popular medium (comics) has begun to tell tales of his granddaughter, Chrissie Claus.

Santa Claus is a legend adults of certain backgrounds and temperaments tell themselves. Of course they tell it to their children, who believe it, but then, as an informal rite of passage, stop believing as they grow older. Later, as adults, they tell themselves that in some way it really is true after all, and that Christmas really is a special, qualitatively different time of year. For many Americans it is outside of their cultural or religious experience: Santa Claus is primarily a Christian tradition. Yet he, and Christmas generally, have become part of the official national culture as well. This can result in deep ambivalence and sometimes resentment among people who do not celebrate Christmas but feel that it is foisted upon them. As a major annual festival, primarily Christian but increasingly secular in nature, Christmas is an interesting example of popular religion, during which the historical, cultural, and economic dimensions of society are framed and validated by the sacred and the spiritual. These values are communicated through the popular media, especially those films that are not only about Christmas, but have become part of the Christmas festival itself.

Conclusion

In this book I have attempted to indicate the enormous quantity and vast array of holiday-oriented consumer goods, particularly media products. I have also tried to show how everyday social life is deeply informed by the sense of season as crystallized in the special calendrical occasions known as holidays. Willis, referring to Adorno, has described capitalism as a "form of consciousness," and it is in this sense that I describe it as the basis of a cultural system in and of itself (see Willis 1991, 9). We would expect our sacred symbols and rituals to validate and reinforce the culture in which they occur. Contemporary American society is a capitalist culture, regardless of whether particular individuals approve. As a result, whatever their histories, our rituals, festivals, and celebrations manifest the capitalist, consumerist society in which they take place. Jameson talks of how in the postmodern situation the terms 'cultural' and 'economic' "collapse back into one another and say the same thing, in an eclipse of the [Marxist] distinction between base and superstructure that has often struck people as significantly characteristic of postmodernism in the first place" (1991, xxi). In this sense, then, the phenomena we have surveyed indicate the postmodern condition: ritual, festival and celebration have become commodified, and social life expresses its relationship to itself, to the cosmos, to time and seasons, through M&Ms, movies, and mystery novels.

This is true as far as it goes, but it must be remembered that while these mass-produced artifacts can be viewed as mere simulacra of directly engaged, participatory ritual and celebration, these objects are used. While these artifacts may function as a substitute for sociability, they are just as often the medium, or the excuse, for it.

For instance, I have conducted research into the ways people who enjoy seasonal comics actually use them and what personal reminiscences about them they may have. Maggie Thompson, who is the editor of *Comics Buyers Guide,* an important weekly newsmagazine in the comics industry, referred to reading seasonal comics as a family tradition she and her late husband (and former coeditor) Don Thompson enjoyed with their children:

> While Don was downstairs, preparing the punch and lighting the candles, and turning on the Christmas lights on Christmas morning, for example, I would read favorite Walt Kelly stories— such as "How Santa Got His Red Suit"—out of *Santa Claus Funnies* and *Christmas with Mother Goose.* Later in the day, Don would sit with Valerie and Stephen to read them such stories as "A Christmas for Shacktown" and "The Golden Christmas Tree," not to mention the story of the duelling steam shovels. Stories tended to be those by Kelly and Barks, but Gollub's wonderful "The Littlest Angel" from *Santa Claus Funnies* was another favorite.
>
> Similarly, while Easter Bunny Don hid the eggs, I would read the kids stories from *Easter with Mother Goose.* These were intrinsic, joyous, shared parts of our holiday celebrations, year after year.

Ryan Ramsey, a student at Iowa State University, wrote me the following:

> I have been an avid reader and collector of comics for over fifteen years. One of my favorite seasonal comic books was an

issue of Marvel's *Bizarre Adventures*. It contained a number of unusual Christmas stories, most having a gruesome twist at the end akin to the E.C. comics of the 1950s. One particular story involved a battle of good vs. evil between Santa Claus and an Anti-Claus. This issue is one of my favorites because it is very atypical of most holiday comics which have a positive and often joyous theme.

In general, I think special holiday issues of comic books stand out for readers because they seem to lie outside a character's normal continuum. Thus, anything can happen in this special setting, which often attracts both regular and occasional readers. Also, the prospects can be very exciting when mixing holiday/seasonal mythical or supernatural beings, i.e., Santa Claus, Halloween monsters, the Easter Bunny, with comic book heroes.

These are two very different answers. Maggie Thompson relates cherished memories of family holiday traditions (using the mass-produced comic books). Ryan Ramsey accounts for his personal taste. Unlike Thompson, he remembers the inversive stories as opposed to the heartwarming Walt Kelly and Carl Barks tales Thompson read to her children. Ramsey also associates the specialness of the holiday comic with the liminality of festivity. The comics themselves offer a "time out of time" (Falassi 1987) for the characters, during which anything can happen, even events not usually found in their regular (but still fantastic) issue stories. He suggests that the mythical, supernatural personas associated with many traditional holidays provide fruitful narrative possibilities when they are brought into contact with the larger-than-life, fictional comic book characters.

The common wisdom is that contemporary calendrical celebrations are debased by commercialism; that there was once a time when good cheer, spirituality, and respect for nature were the motivational forces that underlay such celebrations. While this may be the case, it is hard to demonstrate: most celebrations we are aware of take place in contexts different from but not entirely unlike our own.

Almost always they commemorate mythic, religious, or historical events. The contemporary American celebratory calendar reflects national and global events, and incorporates rites of passage, along with ethnic, religious, family, and regional celebrations, to form a kind of invisible structure for our society. Holy day and holiday celebrations have been sponsored by church and state, by king and commerce (see, for instance, Cressy 1989 and Schmidt 1995). Even in tribal societies, we find the exigencies of real life reflected in rituals and festivals: politics and economics, the validation of power relations and the critique of them.

Rather than seeing holidays as withered in value or entirely corrupted by commercialization, I view them as continuing to possess great significance and power. I would suggest that holidays are of the utmost importance to contemporary, postindustrial, existential, postmodern life. It is perhaps inevitable that as members of society we do not see holidays as forming a structure whereby time, the world, and our places in them are symbolically ordered, in the same way that people do not perceive their own myths as arbitrary. We need to ritualize the flow of time and the place of social groupings and individuals within it. One might disapprove of the underlying ideology that provides the basis of organization, be it religious, political, or economic, but such organizational paradigms, manifested symbolically and ritualistically, are culturally derived and serve social purposes.

Of course, these organizational paradigms (e.g., capitalism, Roman Catholicism, or communism), and the particular ritualized expressions themselves, are contested. Gay groups sue for the right to march in St. Patrick's Day parades. Native American Indians challenge the origin myth or meta-narrative underlying Thanksgiving and hold counter-celebrations, while the emancipation celebrations of African Americans challenge the ideology of the Fourth of July (see Wiggins 1987). The commercial objects examined in this book are products of the dominant American ideology, capitalism, and so reify that system. They are not, as both Bakhtin (1968) and Lane (1981) have suggested, produced from the lower socioeconomic classes and therefore inversive; they come from the top down and so reinforce the social structure as it exists. Handelman would describe the commercial products we have examined as public artifacts related to what he refers to as rituals of presentation, in which the power system is presented as right and natural, merely because it exists (1990). My point in this book is not to endorse the system but rather to suggest that all systems, including ours, are drenched in such seasonality. We are closer to natural events of transition through our symbolic interpretations of them than we may realize.

The can of tomato juice on the shelf during the summer that has an American flag and fireworks on the label represents an attempt to relate a commercial product to a sacred event or period of time, that is, to iconicize it, to create a connection between summer festivities—backyard barbecues and picnics—and tomato juice that seems as correct and enduring as candy canes at Christmas. In this formulation the can of tomato juice is a medium. The label graphics combine images associated with summer celebrations, like the American flag, with the commercial product. The label communicates, or signifies, something new by the combination, an identification that may or may not have existed, and which had not been previously formalized. The purpose is to recreate an otherwise mundane product as a component of festival. This is what Waits refers to as decontamination (1993), and we have seen numerous examples of it throughout this book. Ultimately capitalism is borrowing sacred validation, in this case from the image of the flag, and more generally, by relating commercial products to periods of special, sacred time .

Packaging, as Susan Willis has suggested, is everywhere. It is what she describes as "an unremarked feature of daily life" (1991, 1). Consumer goods packaging is not neutral: it attempts to communicate certain values, ideas, associations, and messages to the consumer. The packaging of commercial goods serves to advertise the product it contains. On the most obvious level, for instance, various genres of popular music have particular graphic styles associated with them. An

Christmas issue magazines from early in the twentieth century.

album jacket, compact disc, or tape whose graphics appear to have been torn from magazines and newspapers and reassembled in a cut-and-paste fashion is mostly likely a punk album; an album using Gothic-inspired calligraphy is more likely heavy metal.

Texts generally are not neutral, whether those texts be album jacket graphics, Hostess doughnut packages, Kleenex boxes, or Thanksgiving cards. Certain images, colors, designs, and symbols were chosen for particular cultural associations they possess. Likewise, the styles in which they are rendered suggest certain readings. However, this does not mean that people necessarily interpret the symbolic forms according to the designer's or the manufacturer's intentions, though they will probably be influenced by them. The graphics might determine the range of interpretations open to the public but not the emotional response. That is, cartoon pilgrims and turkeys on a box of Little Debbie Snack Cakes Pumpkin Delights, on sale in November, indicate that the product is intended as a Thanksgiving item. The graphics suggest that this is a fun item and they appeal to children as well. The immediate frame of the graphic images is an artistic and commercial frame that, along with the temporal frame (the period when the item is on sale) draws attention to the symbolic potential of the pumpkin-based product as having a fit with the harvest imagery of Thanksgiving. Again, the symbols used on the packaging are clearly intended to direct the consumer's attention to the product within. In reality, of course, the consumer will make any number of personally influenced associations, and may or may not interpret the images "correctly," that is, as the industry intended. Nevertheless, the symbols do have preexisting cultural associations, and most people encountering them will be aware of these to at least some extent. A person might see the Pumpkin Delights and decide they would make a good birthday present in December for her friend who has a turkey farm, for instance, but both people involved in this exchange will be cognizant of the overt meaning of the symbolism employed on the package. On the other hand, another person might react with disgust at the commercialization and the obvious attempt to cash in on what is for the individual an important, respectful occasion.

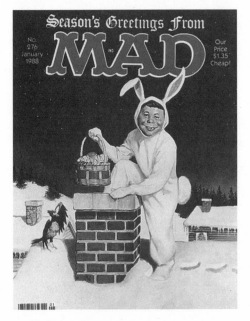

Mad magazine inverts traditional holiday imagery. 1988.

The slip between intention and reception has to do with the qualities of symbols as polysemous and multivocal: symbols can have many meanings simultaneously, and these meanings are expressed through the different properties of the symbolic form, including its color, materials, textures, and so on. Add to this the personal experiences of the individual who encounters them, and the readings seem almost endless. The addition of holiday symbols and designs adds another dimension to the package as frame. Willis is correct to a point when she writes that packaging as a phenomenon remains unremarked in our society, but it is not unnoticed on the level of the individual item. People notice changes in designs, and sometimes consciously purchase something primarily because they like the packaging.

Holiday imagery on a commercial item is especially intended to call attention to itself in ways that "ordinary" packaging is not. That is, Willis is right when she implies that we take packaging for granted, accepting it as a natural rather than a cultural phenomenon. Holiday imagery is meant to appear extraordinary, just as the days they refer to are special, thus relying upon and reinforcing the perception that most packaging is ordinary and natural. Regardless of whether the product contained is in any way different, holiday-oriented packaging suggests that it is special, and temporary (the "summer edition" of Cap'n Crunch, the baseball-oriented Cap'n Crunch's Homerun Crunch, warns, "Available for a limited time only" on the box) in the same way that the holiday or season it refers to is special, sacred, and transitory.

Boxes of Christmas Kleenex tissues are purchased for the special decorator box they come in. These can be displayed as a holiday decoration in their own right. Even unusual items such as Easter Lip Smacker or holiday (Christmas) vacuum freshener are intended to somehow enhance the holiday; to not only be appropriate for it but to become a part of it. The extreme in this kind of thing is seen in the marketing of electric Christmas lights in the shape of M&Ms—the ultimate triumph of commercial marketing, where not only does the commodity become the ritual object, but the ritual object is made in the image and likeness of mass-marketed foods.

Issues of race and gender are important here as well. When we deal in the realm of the supermarket, as I have largely done in the paragraph above and in other sections throughout this book, we are in the female domain. Note that so many of the products mentioned, such as tissues, air freshener, vacuum cleaner freshener, lip balm, and all the foodstuffs can legitimately be considered more likely to be purchased by women. We must assume then that holiday graphics are frequently aimed at women. Foodstuffs, along with other consumer goods, are gendered, even those that ostensibly are aimed at children. It is the parent, most often the mother, who is begged to purchase the item. The selection and preparation of food are generally domestic and female activities, as is the preparation for and maintenance of holiday traditions. These activities are part of what Barbara Myerhoff has termed "domestic religion," which she locates as the cultural property of women (Myerhoff 1978). Commercial products are gendered accordingly. Commercially packaged foods, cleaning products associated with housework, and holidays generally all reside in the domain of the feminine, and there is a conceptual framework, a kind of cultural logic (see Jameson 1991) as to their linkage, though this too is being contested.

As I suggested above, what people actually do with commercial items is something else. At the beginning of this book I referred to a course I teach on holidays and popular culture, and I quoted from a response to a letter of inquiry written by one of my students. Here, at the end of the book, I would like to return to that course to report on an excellent undergraduate research project conducted by Stacy Young. She reported on a family near Akron, Ohio, who have developed some very moving family rituals. Ms. Young interviewed Lois Baker, her youngest daughter, Megan (age twenty-one), and her oldest daughter, Kathy Stewart. The family has had its share of tragedy: Kathy lost two of her children as infants. Interestingly and compellingly, she has incorporated their deaths into her Christmas celebration, as we will see. First, however, we will visit with Megan and examine the ways storebought Christmas ornaments acquire meaning, and how their use is more important than their origin or mode of production.

Megan is the coordinator of the family Christmas tree. She is in charge of all the ornaments, most of which are storebought. Many of these were purchased in a particular store the family frequented during Thanksgiving and summer vacation trips to Pennsylvania:

When we were kids we picked out these real generic ornaments like Fred Flintstone dressed as Santa. Every year we got to pick out an ornament. My mom would get ornaments there too. Everything usually had a date on it. My mother started buying glass balls with dates on them. Now she is into buying Hallmark ornaments that are mechanical, and they also have the date on them. All together I'd say we have a good 450 ornaments. A few of our ornaments are very old. They were my Nana's [on her mother's side of the family] from her tree when she was a girl. They were storebought ornaments. They are tiny. One is a teapot and the other is a violin.

These objects, and the ornaments purchased during family trips as a child, have strong personal meaning for Megan: "Going to that shop was one of my clearest memories from being a kid," she says.

Meanwhile, her mother, Lois, began attending ornament parties, at which friends exchanged commercially produced ornaments as Christmas gifts. Through such communal rituals, these mass-produced objects acquire social and personal meanings. Mrs. Baker says: "We usually went about a week before Christmas. There were at least six couples. We would start at one couple's home to see how their tree was decorated. Each couple bought an ornament. We would exchange ornaments with the couple whose home you'd go to after your own. At each home we would have some kind of snack or desert." Thus, even though the ornaments are mass-produced and storebought, they are an integral part of a neighborhood tradition. Mrs. Baker takes great care to display these gifts on her tree. As Young points out in her paper, the ornament has what she terms an "acquired intention," because it was purchased with a particular individual in mind. "The ornament then takes on personal meaning to its new owner. The ornaments can also trigger memories of a family member like the grandmother whose ornaments hang on their tree. Ornaments on Christmas trees are comparable to pictures and souvenirs that fill the pages of family scrapbooks. Storebought ornaments really can have sentimental value for a family. When the Baker family scans the Christmas tree, they are in essence turning the pages of their memories" (Young 1993).

On the other hand, Kathy, the eldest sister, relishes handmade ornaments. She says:

> I like to sew and do crafts. In college I started embroidering dates onto Christmas ornaments, some doves and angels. In 1984 when Bill and I were just dating, he was into making things out of wood. He would cut the ornaments out for me to paint. That was when we first started making ornaments together. We got married in 1986 and we added a couple of new ornaments then. We went on a trip to Florida and I collected sea shells. I painted them and put ribbons on them and made them into Christmas ornaments. Then I saved flowers from the centerpieces of our wedding. They are ribbon roses, and I place them on our tree. After we were married, Bill's father passed away. I took some flowers from his funeral and put them into a ball inscribed with his name. We put it on the tree where it can be seen so he can be remembered at Christmas. When I lost my babies I took flowers from their funerals and put them into plastic hearts with their names. I also made stockings and ornaments for Randy and the twins [the children who passed away]. Since I lost my babies, I joined a support group. Every year we have a memorial service. We get angels from the group for each baby every year and hang them from the tree to include them in our holiday.

In effect, Kathy makes her Christmas tree a rite-of-passage tree for her family. By transforming the ritual objects of family funerals (which represent unimaginable pain) into Christmas ornaments and displaying these on the family tree, she both deals with her grief and incorporates departed family members into the ongoing life cycle of the family. She and her husband have a healthy daughter now, Catherine. Her happy arrival has also been met with the ornament custom, in this case encompassing both the homemade and storebought traditions in the family. Her grandmother Lois has bought ornaments for

Catherine, and Kathy has made some for her: "I took flowers from when she was born and I put them into a glass ball. I hope someday she will pass down the tradition and make some ornaments of her own." Kathy's tree reflects the joyful as well as the sad rituals of her experience, the rites of passage of birth as well as death. These are all displayed together, along with storebought items that carry memories and kind thoughts from family and friends. The value of these store-bought objects lies not in their intrinsic worth but in the context in which they were acquired and the relationships and shared experiences they represent.

The testimony above reflects the issues of gender referred to earlier. Husband and father are mentioned in passing, but the principal actors, both in the telling and in the incidents recounted, are women in roles as mother, grandmother, sister, aunt, daughter. While men may certainly be the ritual specialists of some families, the above case shows the extent to which the annual calendrical festivals are part of the domestic cultural property of women. Commercial industries recognize this and produce commercial goods pitched at women. When we investigate race and ethnicity, we find some products aimed at specific population groups, such as Cinco de Mayo promotions for both Taco Bell and Corona Beer. Since Corona is Mexican beer, and Taco Bell serves Mexican-derived foods, it makes sense that both would use the national celebration of Mexico's independence symbolically, although the appropriation of this holiday is offensive to many. At some level, however, it also reflects the growing awareness of the

As Americans become increasingly aware of the cultural pluralism of their country, other midwinter celebrations are becoming commercially elaborated. 1992 (Hanukkah); 1994 (Kwanzaa).

fact that a great many Americans are of Hispanic background. And again, there is an inevitability to this kind of cultural appropriation and exploitation in a commercial, consumerist culture. Just as the American flag is frequently used in advertising, so are Mexican American traditions.

Both Kwanzaa and Hanukkah serve as ethnic and religious alternatives or additions to the Christian Christmas. Although Hanukkah is an ancient commemoration, it has been elaborated recently in the United States in a manner directly paralleling the commercialization of Christmas. For instance, Christmas brochures regularly devote pages to Hanukkah items. Along with dreidels, chocolate Hanukkah gelt, and menorahs, items that directly parallel Christmas artifacts such as wrapping paper and countdown calendars resembling Advent calendars are available. One can buy, in effect, Hanukkah versions of familiar Christmas things. In one way this represents a rather cynical reinterpretation of Hanukkah as the Jewish Christmas, a characterization that Jews strongly reject. On the other hand, such merchandising affords the opportunity for Jewish children to engage in activities similar to the festivities

Felix the Cat lights the Hanukiya. Rarely do "funny animals" practice a faith other than Christianity, but as the greeting card industry begins to reflect cultural pluralism, so do some of our familiar cartoon characters.

they find themselves surrounded by every December.

Likewise Kwanzaa, despite its recent origins, has begun to spawn greeting cards. In fact, mass-produced commercial greeting cards with an Afrocentric perspective are appearing for the life-cycle rites of passage as well, such as weddings. These, and perhaps the Black Santas one sees here and there, reflect a true African American popular culture of holidays and celebrations. Furthermore, mass culture, in its demographically based marketing, reflects different groups. A friend of mine told me that for her the Christmas season begins when she plays *The Temptations' Christmas Card* album. Here is music by a African American singing group who had enormous appeal to both African Americans and whites, but certainly are major figures in any canon of Black popular music. Like so many other commercial artists, they too recorded a seasonal album. It is used by this individual as part of an unofficial rite of passage to open the Christmas season. This is the popular use of the mass media, in this case an African American use of African American popular music.

We see more examples of this with the seasonal comics that were described earlier. Some people actively use them as a hallowed aspect of Christmas tradition. This is an example of the commercial artifact becoming (like *A Christmas Carol*) a real component of the holiday. Even more interesting are the thoughts of Shalom (Sholly) Fisch, who has written Christmas comics stories and is an Orthodox Jew. He has written to me and shared his thoughts on the matter:

> Back when I first got into comics, there were no superheroes who were identifiably Jewish. . . . Now, that didn't bother me terribly, because I never really thought about it. Pretty much every superhero was a WASP (as were most of the characters on TV, etc.), so I just took it as a given. Over the years, I developed a soft spot for the Christmas stories that Marvel and DC would publish; the stories were generally warm, upbeat, and a change of pace from the usual. The fact that they often had a Christian slant didn't change the things that I liked about them. I never felt that Christmas stories should be kept out of comics. . . . In the years since then, I've written Christmas, Chanuka, and non-denominational "holiday" stories of my own. (I think Editor Renee Witterstaetter deserves a lot of credit for making sure that the *Marvel Holiday Specials* always include Chanuka as well as Christmas stories.)
>
> I was never bothered by seeing facets of other religions in comics. I'm glad that there are now superheroes who are identi-

fied as Jewish, but I certainly don't think that Judaism should be the only religion represented. And by the same token, I wouldn't want to see us return to a time when every character was Christian. A good story with positive values is a good story with positive values, plain and simple.

Willis argues that "the commodity form [is] the raw material for the meanings that people produce. From this point of view, the most recognizable commodity (what is seen as wholly 'artificial') is somehow freer of past associations and more capable of giving access to alternative meanings" (Willis 1991, 110). From this perspective, people are always making culture: they are active agents rather than passive recipients of social and cultural meanings. Still, a survey of nationally marketed forms and materials reveals that very little is created with racial or ethnic groups in mind. The exceptions, such as those noted above, are transformations of artifacts that represent white middle-class activities and values into artifacts that use the forms (without capturing or appreciating the contents) of other traditions. Perhaps the widespread marketing of St. Patrick's Day as a time when everybody is Irish, with all the attendant merchandising of cute leprechauns, *Erin go bragh* flags (how many people who purchase these know that *Erin go bragh* means "Ireland forever"?), and sexy models in green derby hats offering Lite of the Irish Lite Beer, is the most extreme commercialization of what was once an ethnic and religious celebration in the United States.

Holidays interrelate with the popular media and other aspects of popular, everyday life in several ways. We have looked at the uses of holidays in a variety of popular media: film, television, and print, including magazines, comics, and popular fiction. The schema suggested in chapter 1—that commercial products can be for, about, relevant to, and appropriate for holidays; they may also contain, involve, or use holiday elements without the intention of specifying the artifact as a ritual component of the celebration or festival—can be extended to non-narrative forms as well. Of course, these categories overlap; they move from the specific to the general. Thus, an example of the more general sort can fit the more particular, but the same is not true in reverse. A love movie is appropriate for Valentine's Day, but is not restricted to it, while a movie with a Valentine's Day theme is out of place any time other than the first two weeks of February. Furthermore, new popular holiday artifacts are often produced by adapting preexisting materials from other holidays.

Beyond these issues of commerce lie the more profound issues of celebration. Holidays are welcomed by some, shunned by others; they delight some people and sadden others. They are neither good nor bad in and of themselves. Holiday celebrations are the products of our society, of human behavior, of us, and they magnify all our weaknesses and strengths, our hopes and failures. They are colorful and noisy, joyful and disruptive. They provide the opportunity to tell the world who we are and what we believe in; to challenge authority or to embrace it; and to participate with friends and family in age-old customs and traditions that we continually recreate in new old-fashioned ways.

References

Bakhtin, Mikhail. 1968. *Rabelais and His World.* Translated by Helene Iswolsky. Cambridge, Mass.: MIT Press.

Baum, L. Frank. [1879] 1976. *The Life and Adventures of Santa Claus.* New York: Dover Publications.

Bauman , Richard. 1972. Belsnickling in a Nova Scotia Island Community. *Western Folklore* 31:229–43.

Beck, Ervin. 1982. Children's Guy Fawkes Customs of Sheffield. *Folklore* 95, 2:191–203.

———. 1983. Children's Halloween Customs of Sheffield. *Lore and Language* 3.

———. 1985. Trickster on the Threshold: An Interpretation of Children's Autumn Traditions. *Folklore* 96, 1.

Belk, Russell W. 1993. "Materialism and the Making of Modern American Christmas," in Miller, Daniel, ed. *Unwrapping Christmas.* Oxford: Clarendon Press, 75–104.

Best, Joel, and Gerald T. Horiuchi. 1985. "The Razor Blade in the Apple: The Social Construction of Urban Legends." *Social Problems* 32, no. 5: 488–99.

Brody, Alan. 1969. *The English Mummers and Their Plays.* Philadelphia: Univ. of Pennsylvania Press.

Corwin, Norman. [1942] 1952. *The Plot to Overthrow Christmas.* New York: Henry Holt and Company.

Cressy, David. 1989. *Bonfires and Bells: National Memory and the Protestant Calendar in Elizabethan and Stuart England.* Berkeley: Univ. of California Press.

Cummings, John, and Wendy Bridges. 1985. Sweetest Day Is Sweet Success for Lovers and Businesses Alike. *The BG News,* Fri., Oct. 18, 7.

Davis, Paul. 1990. *The Life and Times of Ebenezer Scrooge.* New Haven, Conn.: Yale Univ. Press.

Dika, Vera. 1990. *Games of Terror: Halloween, Friday the 13th, and the Films of the Stalker Cycle.* London and Toronto: Associated Univ. Presses.

Docherty, David, David Morrison, and Michael Tracy. 1986. "Who Goes to Cinema?" *Sight and Sound* 55.

Falassi, Alessandro, ed. 1987. *Time Out of Time: Essays on the Festival.* Albuquerque: Univ. of New Mexico Press.

Fiske, John. 1989. *Understanding Popular Culture.* Boston: Unwin Hyman.

Frith, Simon. 1988. *Art Into Pop* and *Music for Pleasure: Essays in the Sociology of Pop.* New York: Routledge.

Glassie, Henry. 1968. *Pattern in the Material Folk Culture of the Eastern United States.* Philadelphia: Univ. of Pennsylvania Press.

———. 1972. Folk Art. In *Folklore and Folklife: An Introduction,* edited by Richard Dorson. Chicago: Univ. of Chicago Press, 253–80.

———. 1975. *All Silver and No Brass: An Irish Christmas Mumming.* Bloomington: Indiana Univ. Press.

Golby, J. M., and A. W. Purdue. 1986. *The Making of the Modern Christmas.* Athens: Univ. of Georgia Press.

Grider, Sylvia. 1984. The Razor Blades in Apples Syndrome. In *Perspectives on Contemporary Legend,* edited by Paul Smith. CECTAL Conference Papers Series 34. Sheffield, Eng.: Univ. of Sheffield, 128–40.

Halpert, Herbert, and G. M. Story, eds. 1969. *Christmas Mumming in Newfoundland.* Toronto: Univ. of Toronto Press.

Handelman, Don. 1990. *Models and Mirrors: Towards an Anthropology of Public Events.* Cambridge: Cambridge Univ. Press.

Hobsbawm, Erik, and Terrence Ranger, eds. 1983. *The Invention of Tradition.* Cambridge: Cambridge Univ. Press.

Holt, Tonie, and Valmai Holt. 1987. *I'll Be Seeing You: World War II through Its Picture Postcards.* Ashbourne, Derbyshire, England: Moorland Publishing Co.

Humphrey, Theodore C., and Lin T. Humphrey. 1988. *"We Gather Together": Food and Festival in American Life.* Ann Arbor, Mich.: UMI Research Press.

Izod, John. 1988. *Hollywood and the Box Office 1895–1986.* New York: Columbia Univ. Press.

Jameson, Fredric. 1991. *Postmodernism or, the Cultural Logic of Late Capitalism.* Durham, N.C.: Duke Univ. Press.

Kahn, Roger, 1972. *The Boys of Summer.* New York: Harper and Row.

Keller, Morton. 1968. *The Art and Politics of Thomas Nast.* New York: Oxford Univ. Press.

Lane, Christel. 1981. *The Rites of Rulers: Ritual in Industrial Society—The Soviet Case.* Cambridge: Cambridge Univ. Press.

Lévi-Strauss, Claude. 1993. Father Christmas Executed. In *Unwrapping Christmas,* edited by Daniel Miller. Oxford: Clarendon Press, 38–51.

MacAloon, John J. 1984. Olympic Games and the Theory of Spectacle in Modern Societies. In *Rite, Drama, Festival, Spectacle: Rehearsals Towards a Theory of Cultural Performance,* edited by John J. MacAloon. Philadelphia: ISHI, 241–80.

Marsh, Dave, and Steve Propes. 1993. *Merry Christmas, Baby: Holiday Music from Bing to Sting.* Boston: Little, Brown and Co.

Milberg, David A. 1993. Saluting Summer: Pop Music's Second Most Favorite Time of the Year. *DISCoveries* (July): 31–35.

Miller, Daniel, ed. 1993. *Unwrapping Christmas.* Oxford: Clarendon Press.

Myerhoff, Barbara. 1978. *Number Our Days.* New York: Simon and Schuster.

Paine, Albert Bigelow. 1904. *Th. Nast: His Period and His Pictures.* New York: Macmillan and Co.

Papson, Stephen. 1986. From Symbolic Exchange to Bureaucratic Discourse: The Hallmark Greeting Card. *Theory, Culture, and Society* 3, no. 2, 99–111.

Real, Michael. 1977. *Mass-Mediated Culture.* Englewood Cliffs, N.J.: Prentice-Hall.

Sadler, A. W. 1994. The Seasonal Context of Halloween: Vermont's Unwritten Law. In *Halloween and Other Festivals of Death and Life,* edited by Jack Santino. Knoxville: Univ. of Tennessee Press, 170–86.

Santino, Jack. 1983. Halloween in America: Contemporary Customs and Performances. *Western Folklore* 62, no. 1, 1–20.

———. 1986. The Folk Assemblage of Autumn: Tradition and Creativity in Halloween Folk Art. In *Folk Art and Art Worlds,* edited by Simon Bronner and John Michael Vlach. Ann Arbor, Mich.: UMI Research Press, 151–69.

———. 1992. Yellow Ribbons and Seasonal Flags: The Folk Assemblage of War. *Journal of American Folklore* 105, no. 415, 19–33.

———. 1994. *All Around the Year: Holidays and Celebrations in American Life.* Urbana: Univ. of Illinois Press.

Schmidt, Leigh Eric. 1991. The Commercialization of the Calendar: American Holidays and the Culture of Consumption, 1870–1930. *Journal of American History* (Dec.), 887–916.

———. 1995. *Consumer Rites: The Buying and Selling of American Holidays.* Princeton, N.J.: Princeton Univ. Press.

Smith, Robert Jerome. 1972. The Structure of Esthetic Response. In *Towards New Perspectives in Folklore,* edited by Americo Paredes and Richard Bauman. Austin: Univ. of Texas Press, 68–79.

Stam, Robert. 1988. Mikhail Bakhtin and Left Cultural Critique. In *Postmodernism and Its Discontents,* edited by E. Ann Kaplan. London: Verso, 116–45.

Turner, Victor. 1967. Betwixt and Between: The Liminal Period in *Rites de Passage.* In *The Forest of Symbols.* Ithaca, N. Y.: Cornell Univ. Press, 93–111.

Waits, William B. 1993. *The Modern Christmas in America: A Cultural History of Gift Giving.* New York: New York Univ. Press.

Weiser, Francis X. 1952. *The Christmas Book.* New York: Harcourt, Brace and Co.

Wiggins, William. 1987. *O Freedom: Afro-American Emancipation Celebrations.* Knoxville: Univ. of Tennessee Press.

Willis, Susan. 1991. *A Primer for Daily Life.* London: Routledge.

Young, Stacy. 1993. Magic: The Life of a Christmas Tree. Unpublished paper, Bowling Green State Univ.

Index

New *Old-Fashioned Ways* was designed and typeset on a MacIntosh computer system using PageMaker software. The text is set in Gill Sans, a typeface designed by Eric Gill in 1929. Chapter titles are set in Dolmen, a distinctive sans serif type with widely contrasting thick and thin strokes. This book was designed by Todd Duren, and composed by Angela Stanton. The recycled paper used in this book is designed for an effective life of at least three hundred years.